ORCA **Think**

Question, connect and take action to become better citizens with a brighter future. Now that's smart thinking!

SUPERPOWER?

The Wearable-Tech Revolution

Elaine Kachala

illustrated by Belle Wuthrich

ORCA BOOK PUBLISHERS

Published in Canada and the United States in 2022 by Orca Book Publishers.
orcabook.com

Library and Archives Canada Cataloguing in Publication
Title: Superpower? : the wearable-tech revolution / Elaine Kachala ; illustrated by Belle Wuthrich.
Names: Kachala, Elaine, author. | Wuthrich, Belle, 1989- illustrator.
Series: Orca think ; 7.
Description: Series statement: Orca think ; 7 | Includes bibliographical references and index.
Identifiers: Canadiana (print) 20210365897 | Canadiana (ebook) 2021036596X |
ISBN 9781459828278 (hardcover) | ISBN 9781459828285 (PDF) | ISBN 9781459828292 (EPUB)
Subjects: LCSH: Wearable computers—Juvenile literature. |
LCSH: Wearable technology—Juvenile literature.
Classification: LCC QA76.592 .K33 2022 | DDC j004.167—dc23

Library of Congress Control Number: 2021949082

Summary: This illustrated nonfiction book for middle-grade readers explores the history, development, applications and ethics of wearable technology.

Orca Book Publishers is committed to reducing the consumption of nonrenewable resources in the production of our books. We make every effort to use materials that support a sustainable future.

Orca Book Publishers gratefully acknowledges the support for its publishing programs provided by the following agencies: the Government of Canada, the Canada Council for the Arts and the Province of British Columbia through the BC Arts Council and the Book Publishing Tax Credit.

Cover and interior artwork by Belle Wuthrich
Design by Dahlia Yuen
Edited by Kirstie Hudson

Printed and bound in Canada.

25 24 23 22 • 1 2 3 4

To Michael, whose unconditional love and support mean everything—the words "thank you" don't seem to be enough. To Nicole and Allison, whose persistence and courageousness are my inspiration.

Motion-capture technology (or mocap for short) is a way to record people's movements digitally. It's used in film, animation, gaming, healthcare, education and more. This person is wearing body sensors to capture their movements, which are reproduced in real time with software and cloud processing.

ANDREY BURMAKIN/
SHUTTERSTOCK.COM

Contents

FIRE
DEPT.
MEDI

Introduction

CAUTION! MOVE SLOW AND THINK HUMAN

Did you know you're among the most technologically literate generation *ever* to live on this planet? You will shape the future!

Did you also know that technology is developing faster now than at any other time in history? We're in the midst of a Fourth Industrial Revolution because of how ***artificial intelligence (AI)***, robotics, the ***Internet of Things (IoT)*** and more are reshaping the world. These technologies are powering remarkable developments in so many areas of our lives, including wearable computing. *Wearable* means just what you'd expect—technology that's on, in or attached to your body. When people wear technology, it changes them. It changes what they can see and do, and how they think, communicate and experience the world. More and more wearables are giving humans superpowers. Super strength. Super hearing. Super vision. Super expression. Super connection. Super intelligence!

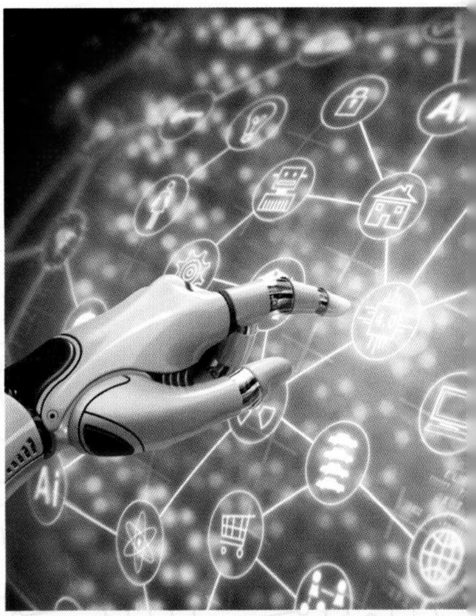

Like earlier industrial revolutions, the Fourth Industrial Revolution is transforming society. But this time the changes are unlike anything that's happened before. Experts warn of limitless possibilities—good and bad. The future's up to us!

EZPS/SHUTTERSTOCK.COM

Wearable technologies can empower people to live better lives. I work in the health field, and I've seen the amazing benefits. Brain-computer interfaces (BCIs) are helping kids with severe physical disabilities move and communicate. And virtual reality (VR) is reducing loneliness for older adults. Still, there are some things to worry about.

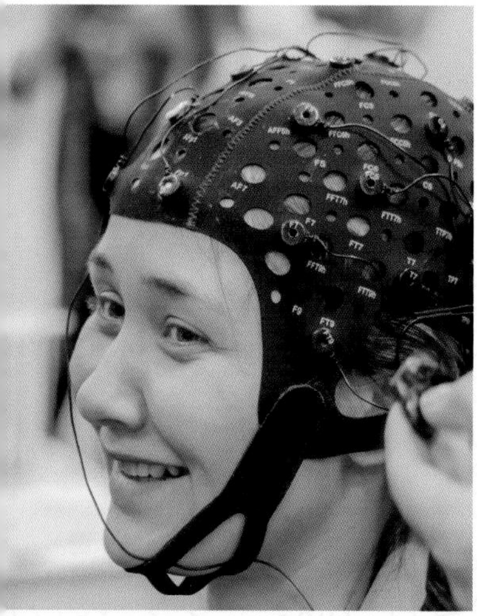

BCIs are one of the most advanced technologies for helping young people who can't use speech to communicate or need assistive devices to move. BCIs link a person's brain with a device such as a keyboard. Brain signals control the device.

ZYABICH/SHUTTERSTOCK.COM

What if some people have technology to help them and others don't? What if wearables are putting people's ***data*** privacy at risk? What if devices aren't fully tested for safety?

I started noticing the news headlines about what was happening in the tech industry. "Hackers easily track kids!" "Cheap ***sensors*** create security risks!" "Companies sell users' data without their knowing!"

I learned that some creators get caught up in a "move fast and break things" culture. It's about innovating fast, getting products out there and not taking enough time to think through how the technologies are affecting people's lives.

More news. One day BCIs could make telepathy possible. And VR? It could change our perception of reality. Some of this terrific tech could have terrifying impacts! The same technologies that help and heal us also raise tricky questions. I wondered, how do ***designers***, engineers and scientists guard against technology's dark side when they're inventing? I did more research and talked to experts, including young inventors your age.

In this book, you'll learn about the wearable-tech revolution. And you'll meet experts who are striving for responsible design. They're on a mission to head off problems before the technology's out there causing harm. They know superpowers can become super problems. And they don't want the dangers to stamp out the incredible benefits.

You'll discover the pros and cons of wearables. Because when it comes to buying, using and designing our ***smart devices***, we make choices. These choices will determine how wearable technology shapes our lives.

Technologies are tools made and used by people. We *do* have a say in how they advance.

Caution! Move slow and think human.

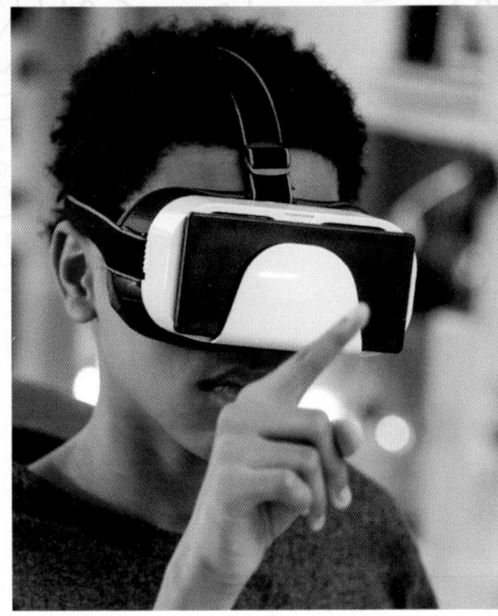

Gaming and learning in VR is a blast. But choose your VR experiences carefully—your brain thinks they're real!

SDI PRODUCTIONS/GETTY IMAGES

Augmented reality (AR) applications help us learn about ourselves and keep track of our busy lives. But is our personal information safe?

YAGI-STUDIO/GETTY IMAGES

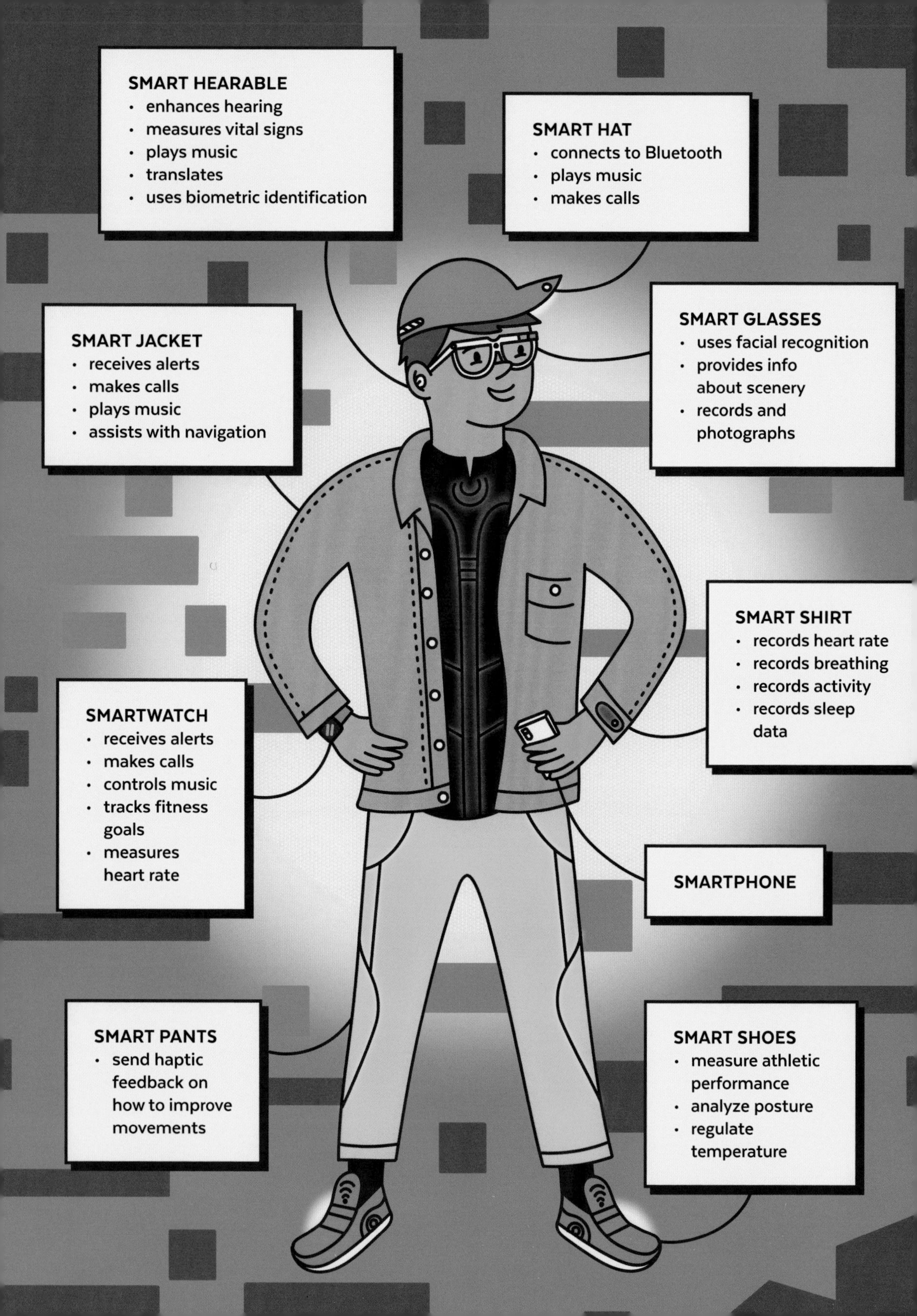
SMART HEARABLE
• enhances hearing
• measures vital signs
• plays music
• translates
• uses biometric identification
SMART HAT
• connects to Bluetooth
• plays music
• makes calls
SMART JACKET
• receives alerts
• makes calls
• plays music
• assists with navigation
SMART GLASSES
• uses facial recognition
• provides info about scenery
• records and photographs
SMART SHIRT
• records heart rate
• records breathing
• records activity
• records sleep data
SMARTWATCH
• receives alerts
• makes calls
• controls music
• tracks fitness goals
• measures heart rate
SMARTPHONE
SMART PANTS
• send haptic feedback on how to improve movements
SMART SHOES
• measure athletic performance
• analyze posture
• regulate temperature

One

Our Wearable World

SOCIETY'S NEXT TECH REVOLUTION

Our world is exploding with wearables. Researchers think that by 2030 over 700 million smartwatches will have been sold worldwide. You might have one already or know someone with one of these devices. Until now they've been the most popular kind of wearable. But that's changing with the next generation of devices. We won't be strapping wearables only onto our wrists!

Our brains, skin, eyes, ears and other body parts, and our clothing, are becoming the new ways we'll connect with technology. Robotic suits are making us stronger. Immersive technologies such as augmented reality (AR) and virtual reality (VR) are changing how we learn, work and play. And brain-computer interfaces (BCIs) are helping us control objects with our thoughts.

Wearable computers are boosting our human capabilities. They're becoming extensions of our bodies to help us think, move, communicate, control our emotions and more.

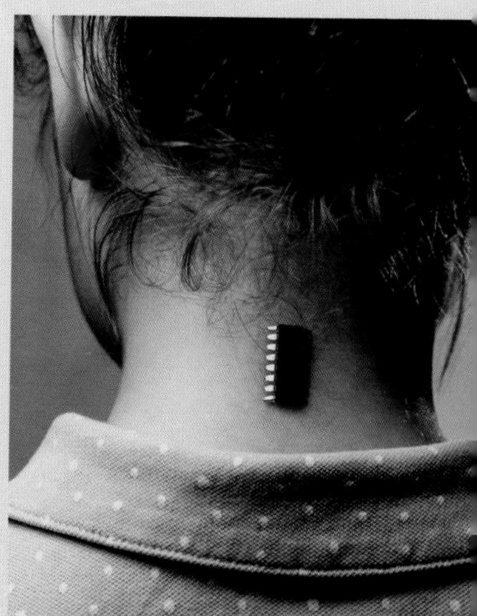

Tagged! Microchips implanted under our skin could store information about our identities and behaviors and could connect to the IoT. Should we get them?
ALEXEY GALUTVA/SHUTTERSTOCK.COM

We're acquiring superpowers and, possibly, changing who we are as human beings.

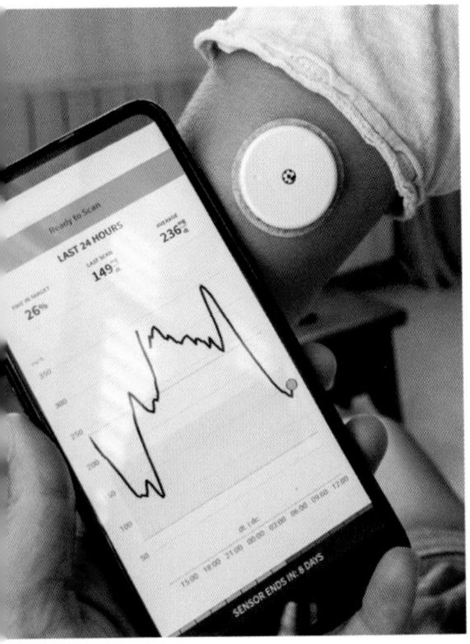

Continuous glucose monitors track blood sugar (glucose) levels throughout the day and night. A sensor worn under the skin transmits levels to a device such as a smartphone. People with diabetes can easily know if their level is too high or low.
ARTUR DEBAT/GETTY IMAGES

WHAT IS WEARABLE TECHNOLOGY?

It's a Computer!

Is a wearable a computer? Yes! Wearables are electronic devices that can store, retrieve and process data. At the core of wearable technology is a computer system. Often the computer is part of the wearable itself. If it's not, then the wearable transmits data that is processed by a computer. Some wearables process data using more than one computer, such as a smartwatch that connects to an app on a smartphone and ***cloud computing*** (computing accessed through the internet). Hardware, software and connections—wearables need them all in order to work. The terms *wearable technology*, *wearable computing* and *wearables* mean the same thing.

Approach. Swipe. Enter! 5G is a game changer for connectivity. It's the fifth generation of mobile networks. 5G has ultra-wideband for faster uploads and ultra-low latency (lag) to support smoother connectivity across more devices.

WEIQUAN LIN/GETTY IMAGES

Sensors are important pieces of hardware. They collect data that is processed and uploaded to the internet via a mobile network, ***Wi-Fi*** or ***Bluetooth***. ***Algorithms*** turn data from the sensors into information people can use. And the data is stored on a personal hard drive, at a storage facility or in the cloud.

Wearables need connections to a smart environment to produce useful information. Most wearable technology is part of the Internet of Things (IoT). The IoT is a system of connected smart devices that can gather, analyze, send and receive data via the internet. This system allows for speedy data transmission, storage and way-more-powerful data processing than a wearable device could do on its own. IoT is at the heart of how our smart devices learn about us and figure out how to work better.

TECH_BYTE

Sensors Are the Secret

Wearable technology relies on sensors to gather information from the body and its surroundings. There are many different types of sensors, geared toward what information is being picked up. For example, GPS is a standard sensor in smartwatches for tracking location. So are sensors to measure heart rate. Immersive technology devices, like VR goggles, rely on combinations of sensors that capture and measure movement, rotation, twist, depth, pressure and more. Electronic skin patches use sensors to measure ***electrolytes*** in sweat.

It's Personal!

Wearables are computers, but they're different from desktops or laptops, tablets or handheld devices because they live on, in or attached to people's bodies. They're intensely personal.

TECH_BYTE

AI Makes Wearables Smarter

An ***algorithm*** is a set of steps that a computer follows to complete a task. Complicated algorithms are designed to allow computers to learn on their own. That's called *machine learning*. Computers learn by recognizing patterns in data and from experience (like playing games). Machine learning means that algorithms can change and create new algorithms as the computer learns new information.

AI is the ability to learn and improve on the basis of new data, without human intervention. AI means that wearables can process massive amounts of complicated data from sensors and deliver more useful information to wearers. Our AI systems are sharing more and more information—they keep becoming smarter and are learning faster and faster.

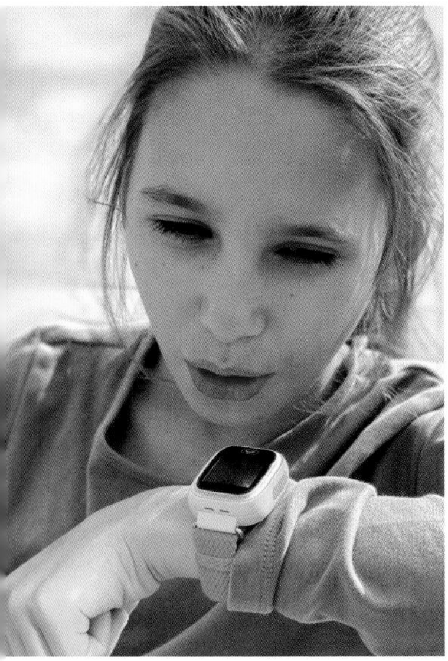

"I'm lost—how do I get home?"
CASARSAGURU/GETTY IMAGES

It's about Humans and Machines as Partners!

Hey, I'm hands-free! I can multitask.

"Always on! Always ready! Always accessible!" That's the point of wearables, says Steve Mann. He's an inventor in Toronto who started the field of wearable computing.

Wearables can boost our hearing, sight, thought, memory, movement and other abilities without our having to stop what we're doing to turn them on. They work as extensions of our bodies and minds. It means we're entering into a new relationship with computers. This might not seem like a big deal, but it is.

Wearable computing helps us think differently about how we want to live with machines.

Some people think that AI is replacing humans with computers. In some ways, this is true. For example, a robot in a factory could take over a human's job. Programmers write algorithms—***code*** that tells computers what to do—and presto, computers can do tasks or solve problems with no human needed!

Many people think we can't let this happen. People have intelligence and imagination. They're kind and caring. We want computers to help us do things better, not be the boss.

Some people feel wearables can help. For example, robotic suits called exoskeletons can give people extra strength to do the same job but better, so people won't lose their jobs. Smart glasses with AR can provide workers with "how to" instructions so they can learn how to do new things in real time more safely. With wearables, humans and computers are partners. They're working together to do jobs better than either could do on their own.

Mann thought about boosting human intelligence and abilities when he invented wearables in the 1970s. He and professors Marvin Minsky and Ray Kurzweil came up with the idea of ***humanistic intelligence (HI)***. It's the whole idea behind wearable computing—helping humans to be smarter and better.

Smart glasses with AR help us learn more about the world.

RYANJLANE/GETTY IMAGES

HI means humans are designed into the computer's decision-making ***loop***—it's called "human-in-the-loop" computing. There's a back-and-forth between the human and the device. A person thinks or does something (human input). Then, with AI, the computer learns about what the person wants and helps them achieve it (output). This happens over and over. In this way, the human and AI work together to solve problems and achieve goals.

Wearable computing is "way more than just a 'wearable' and a 'computer,'" says Mann, because what happens when they come together is remarkable. When HI and AI join forces, three things happen. The wearable works better. People's intelligence and abilities improve. And here's the kicker—it might be our only chance to make sure that computers don't take over and outsmart us.

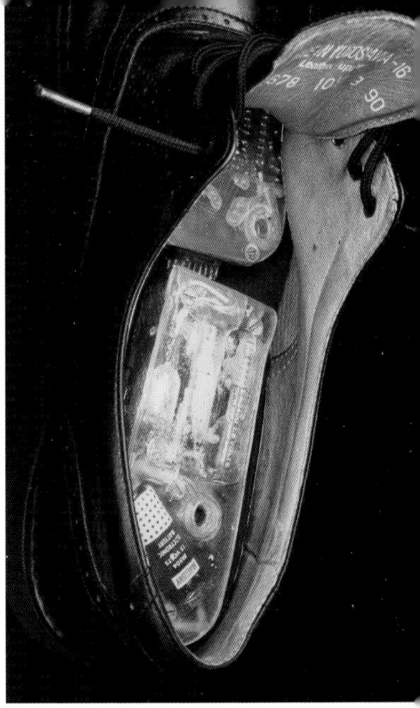

Wires connect microswitches in the toes of these shoes to a small computer worn around the waist and speakers in the ears. The inventors trained their big toes to operate the switches to time the roulette wheel and ball as they spin, proving it was possible to "beat the casino."

STEVE MANN (PHOTO TAKEN WITH THE WEARCOMP SYSTEM)

WEARABLES HAVE A LONG HISTORY

For centuries people have imagined ways to augment their abilities. The earliest recorded use of eyeglasses was in the 13th century. Peter Henlein invented the pocket watch in the 16th century to help people keep track of time. But most experts agree the use of modern wearables begins in 1961. That's when inventors Edward Thorp and Claude Shannon put a computer in a shoe.

These two math professors and gadget lovers with a sense of humor built a computer for one purpose—to win at a casino roulette game. It could predict where the ball would land.

But it was Mann who first developed complex wearable computers with many applications. He's recognized as the Father of Wearable Computing. Since Thorp, Shannon and Mann, many great thinkers and innovators helped pave the way for today's complex wearables.

MOVE SLOW + THINK HUMAN

Hardware + Software + Human = Cyborg

Once humans and computers were separate. But with wearables, we have technological parts. Our bodies and minds are merging with machines for superhuman intelligence and ability. More than just the next tech revolution, wearables may be the next step in human evolution too.

TECH_BYTE

Milestones in Modern Wearable Computing

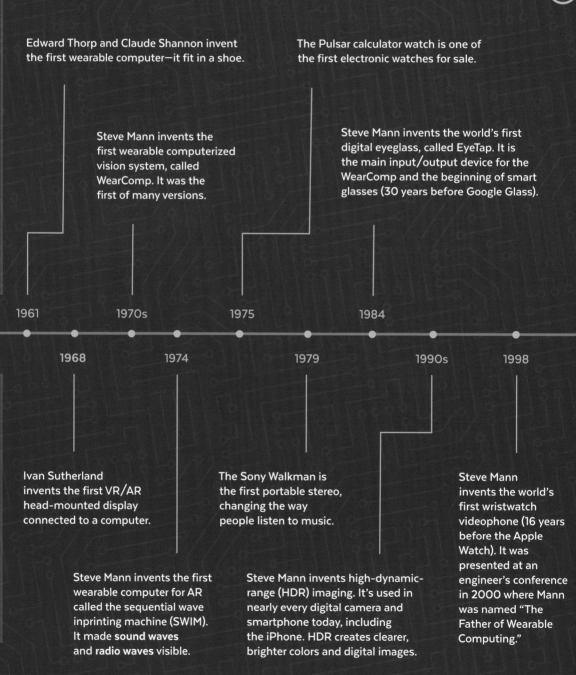

1961
Edward Thorp and Claude Shannon invent the first wearable computer—it fit in a shoe.

1968
Ivan Sutherland invents the first VR/AR head-mounted display connected to a computer.

1970s
Steve Mann invents the first wearable computerized vision system, called WearComp. It was the first of many versions.

1974
Steve Mann invents the first wearable computer for AR called the sequential wave inprinting machine (SWIM). It made **sound waves** and **radio waves** visible.

1975
The Pulsar calculator watch is one of the first electronic watches for sale.

1979
The Sony Walkman is the first portable stereo, changing the way people listen to music.

1984
Steve Mann invents the world's first digital eyeglass, called EyeTap. It is the main input/output device for the WearComp and the beginning of smart glasses (30 years before Google Glass).

1990s
Steve Mann invents high-dynamic-range (HDR) imaging. It's used in nearly every digital camera and smartphone today, including the iPhone. HDR creates clearer, brighter colors and digital images.

1998
Steve Mann invents the world's first wristwatch videophone (16 years before the Apple Watch). It was presented at an engineer's conference in 2000 where Mann was named "The Father of Wearable Computing."

2000

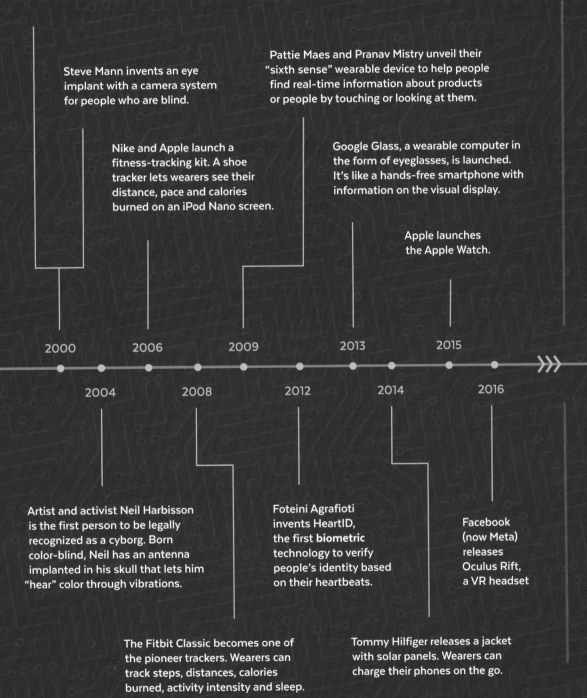

The Industrial Clothing Division at Levi's merges clothes and technology. A conductible jacket has a mobile phone, MP3 player, headphones and a button for wearers to switch between applications.

Steve Mann invents an eye implant with a camera system for people who are blind.

2004

Artist and activist Neil Harbisson is the first person to be legally recognized as a cyborg. Born color-blind, Neil has an antenna implanted in his skull that lets him "hear" color through vibrations.

2006

Nike and Apple launch a fitness-tracking kit. A shoe tracker lets wearers see their distance, pace and calories burned on an iPod Nano screen.

2008

The Fitbit Classic becomes one of the pioneer trackers. Wearers can track steps, distances, calories burned, activity intensity and sleep.

2009

Pattie Maes and Pranav Mistry unveil their "sixth sense" wearable device to help people find real-time information about products or people by touching or looking at them.

2012

Foteini Agrafioti invents HeartID, the first **biometric** technology to verify people's identity based on their heartbeats.

2013

Google Glass, a wearable computer in the form of eyeglasses, is launched. It's like a hands-free smartphone with information on the visual display.

2014

Tommy Hilfiger releases a jacket with solar panels. Wearers can charge their phones on the go.

2015

Apple launches the Apple Watch.

2016

Facebook (now Meta) releases Oculus Rift, a VR headset

CYBORG CELEBRITY

Steve Mann is an inventor, scientist, engineer, artist, designer, activist and more. He has been called a modern-day Leonardo da Vinci. And it all began when he was four years old!

As a kid, Mann was taught how to weld by his grandfather. Welders wear special goggles to protect their eyes from blindingly bright light. But they're not comfortable, and it's hard to see things around you. This experience led Mann to wonder about inventing technology that would improve people's vision.

When he was 12 years old, Mann built his first wearable computer. He called it the SWIM. It was a wand with lights powered by a wearable amplifier and switching system. As you waved it around in space, it let you see radio and sound waves not visible to the human eye. It was the first AR device because you could see these waves layered on the real world. The wand is on display at the National Gallery in Ottawa.

Christina and Stephanie Mann view the first wearable computer their dad invented in 1974—the SWIM. It makes sound and radio waves visible.
STEVE MANN

Mann's childhood fascination with technology led him to study engineering. He became a professor in the Department of Electrical and Computer Engineering at the University of Toronto and specialized in wearable computing. He went on to invent hundreds of smart wearables.

The world's first wristwatch videophone was invented in 1998 by Steve Mann. It was able to capture, send and receive video over the internet. And it had a secret function that concealed the videoconferencing window, so it looked like an ordinary watch.

STEVE MANN

From Inventor to Cyborg

Mann tested his inventions on himself. They became part of his body, and he became an electronic device. People started calling him "the world's first ***cyborg***."

"I live in two worlds, real space and ***cyberspace***," he says.

The WearComp ***prototypes*** of the 1970s, 1980s and 1990s were huge and clunky. People were shocked to see Mann walking around with a head-mounted display, antennae, a welded-steel frame and wires around his body. He said people didn't like him because of how he looked. Or maybe they didn't like what he represented—"a cyborg in a frightening, changing world," he says.

But Mann didn't care! He had a computer, camera, telephone and videophone functions, all on his body.

Steve Mann's wearable computer inventions evolved over the years.

STEVE MANN AND WEBB CHAPPELL (SECOND FROM RIGHT)

ɜve Mann wears his EyeTap digital
ɜglass in 1999.
EVE MANN

As the prototypes evolved and became smaller, he looked less robotic. Cyborg living became easier. Not only was the gear more comfortable to wear, but people became more accepting.

This technology was incredibly empowering. He could roam the city hands-free while talking to people, taking pictures, answering emails and calls or taking notes. It was like having a desktop computer and more strapped to his body.

Mann saw the world through a video lens. He could filter out billboards or other information that he didn't want to see. And he discovered that having images frozen in space in front of his eyes helped him remember places and faces. If he was lost, he could transmit images to his web page, then browse to find his way back. And he could share his experiences firsthand with friends and family in real time.

There was something else too. Surveillance cameras were becoming common in big cities to prevent crime. They were in banks, stores, restaurants and on the streets so that police, store owners or other authorities could watch and record citizens. Mann said it was strange when he realized that cameras were watching and recording him. He wondered about his privacy rights. Why shouldn't he too be able to watch in order to protect himself? He could with his WearComp!

Someone once smashed their car into Mann's house and sped off. Luckily, Mann was wearing his WearComp. He caught the criminal on camera and reported him to the police. True story!

Mann called this experience of also being able to watch "sousveillance." It's like the opposite of surveillance. Sousveillance means watching from below, and it gives power back to people.

'his drawing is by Stephanie,
steve Mann's six-year-old daughter.
TEVE MANN AND STEPHANIE MANN

Living as Cyborgs

Surveillance is an invasion of privacy, but sousveillance can be too. After all, says Mann, "now I can watch you. And if you have a WearComp, you can watch me back!"

Mann realized that the WearComp let him live a freer and safer life. His experiences got him thinking about its unlimited possibilities to help people.

These days he and his team are designing smart eyeglasses called Blueberry. They "look like ordinary eyeglasses," says Mann. "But they have the world's most advanced brain-computer interface in them." They can help people relax, focus and remember. The glasses have brain-sensing technology that can understand how we feel and a camera that shows what's going on around us. These features mean that the glasses can provide real-time information to the person wearing them. Then people can adjust what they're doing, like taking a break, going outside and getting some exercise.

Blueberry is an example of humanistic intelligence (HI) and involves human-in-the-loop design. The team is also working on other devices that will help people with vision problems.

With every invention, Mann thinks about how to create safe, secure designs, how the technology will affect people and what it means to live together as cyborgs.

Police officers wear body cameras to watch and record citizens at a protest. But what if they edit out details that tell the whole story about what happened and arrest people unfairly?

JOHN GOMEZ/SHUTTERSTOCK.COM

Long-exposure photographs of Christina wearing the Blueberry eyeglass. Mann's Metavision system shows what the eyeglass "sees" (senses). Metavision is important because it helps Mann build smart eyeglasses with the right balance between privacy, surveillance and sousveillance.

STEVE MANN AND CHRISTINA MANN

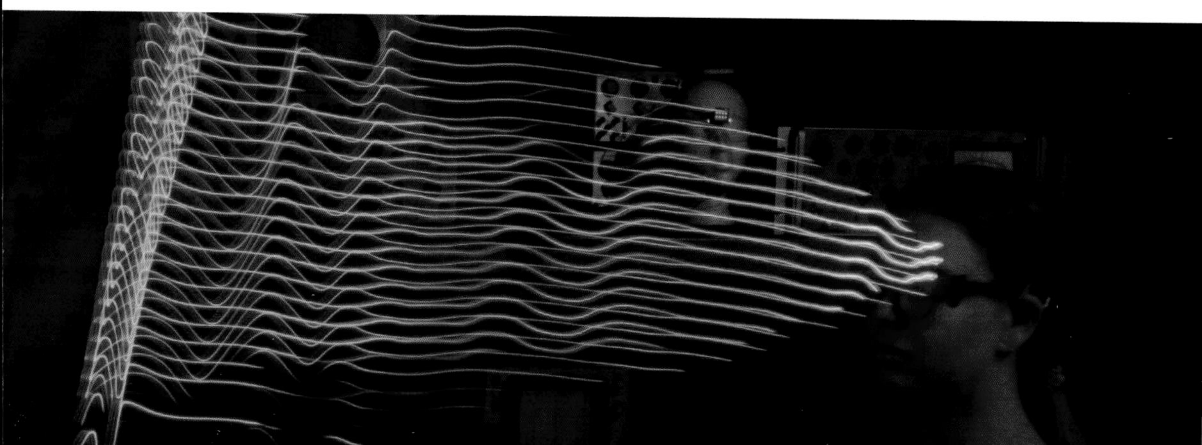

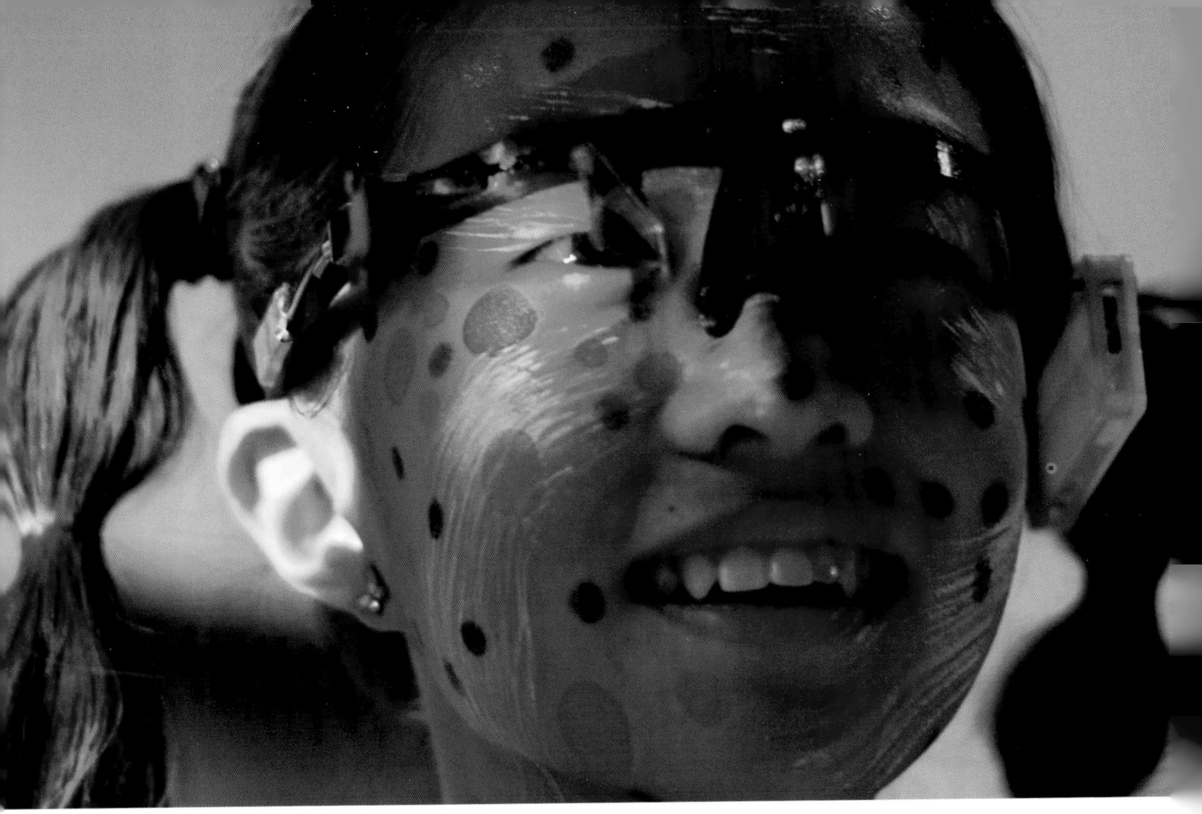

This picture shows Steve Mann's 2017 EyeTap design. You can wear the eyeglass at a sports stadium to follow your favorite team player and have EyeTap display a player's statistics, such as batting average. EyeTap can also superimpose the ball's predicted trajectory on top of visual reality.
ALEX MURRAY-LESLIE

"CyberMan's" Advice

Mann says wearables can improve our lives, but when you put technology on people, it changes them and the world. By augmenting our abilities, wearables change what we can see and do, and how we think, communicate and experience the world.

When we upgrade ourselves with machine parts, this brings new problems. So we'll need rules for a new way of living together. That's why Mann has been working with others to develop a code of ethics for human augmentation.

The code means that people inventing and building technologies have a responsibility. They must look at the effect technology has on people. How does it help or harm us?

If inventors keep in mind the idea of HI, we'll all be safer. HI is a vital force against AI. We can't lose decision-making control to computers. And we can't let computers take over all of our abilities.

Realizing that we live in a world of interconnected things, where smart devices are watching us and collecting our data, the code says we need to be able to watch too. Sousveillance! And this means we must all pledge to respect each other's privacy.

"You're a cyborg too," says Mann. All humans are. And it would be dangerous to pretend this isn't true. Think about how we improve our eyesight with glasses or restore lost limbs with ***prostheses***. And don't smartphones feel like extensions of our minds and bodies? It's interesting how our acceptance of technology happens gradually. Sometimes we don't even notice how much we've changed.

Mann's optimistic about cyborg living but says we need to have an honest discussion about wearable computing.

Wearables open up a world of opportunities to connect with friends and family and improve your abilities.
HQUALITY/SHUTTERSTOCK.COM

DINO PARK TOURS
DINO•TOURS

Two

Wearables Are Changing How We Live

Wearables—they're on us, in us and connected to everything around us. They're not only cool gadgets. They're sophisticated devices that are becoming part of our minds and bodies. And they're changing how we live, learn, work and play. Sometimes technologies are so much a part of our lives that we hardly notice them. Have you spotted changes in your life because of wearables?

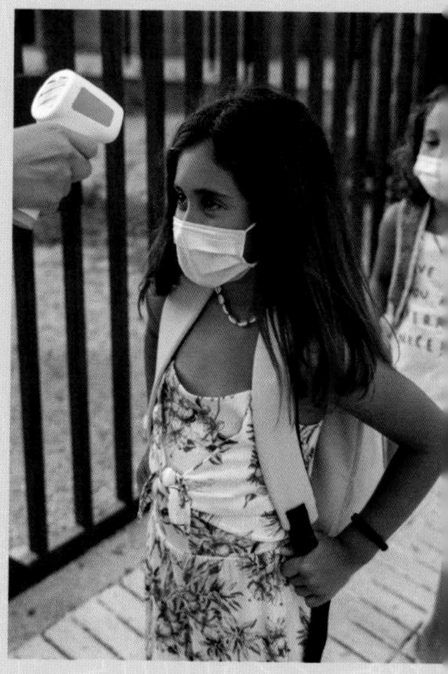

Temperature checks are one way of screening for COVID-19.
JAVIER ZAYAS PHOTOGRAPHY/GETTY IMAGES

TRACKING PEOPLE AND PANDEMICS

STOP! You're dangerously close.

In 2020 the COVID-19 pandemic took over our world. Life changed for everyone. To limit its spread, we couldn't go to school or work or meet up with family and friends. We had to wear masks and wash our hands a zillion times a day. And we had to stay six feet (about two meters) apart.

acial recognition, age, location, family istory—social-distancing technologies an capture it all and more!

ACOBCHUK/GETTY IMAGES

Research and development of wearables for social distancing exploded. What if a device could alert you if someone was too close? Or tell you how long they had been in your safety zone? Could the device prompt you to wear a mask or wash your hands? Could it detect and track the virus's symptoms?

Wearables may be a useful social-distancing tool, but there are problems.

According to a tech advisory company called Gartner there isn't enough proof they are effective or safe. And since wearables must collect personal data in order to function, most devices create privacy concerns. When did you go to the bathroom? What did you buy for lunch? Whom did you eat with? Are we willing to let governments, schools, workplaces and others access this data and track our lives? Do we have to trade privacy for health?

Safe Solutions? Young Inventor Explores Wearable Designs

Christina Mann says she's "a natural-born maker, eager to become an engineer!" When COVID-19 hit, this young inventor got to work with the team at MannLab Canada (yes, the Father of Wearable Computing is Christina's dad!).

What if we each stayed inside a bubble ball filled with fresh filtered air? Nope, it can't fit through doorways. What if we each wore a long-spiked collar? Christina is exploring even the craziest ideas. "Step one in any invention is to define the problem by expanding your thinking about the situation," she says.

She also says we need social-distancing technology that does two things. One, it should help people know if they're keeping the proper distance from one another. Two, it should encourage proper social distancing. But we don't want a device that creates other problems, like putting people's privacy at risk.

The lab began with some fun and crazy prototypes. First they made wooden collars, then 3D printed ones. They tested and made adjustments.

Christina uses engineering, science and art to invent and build solutions. The final design for her social-distancing tool is a collar with sonars that detect when someone's within six feet (about two meters), from any angle. Then it vibrates to warn the user. And it includes black and green lights. The closer the intruder, the brighter the green. It's a device that's safe and trustworthy—and no one's data is tracked.

A bubble ball? A spiked collar? Finally, a 3D-printed prototype. Christina Mann constructed and tested different designs to spark discussion about COVID-19 and social issues and create practical technologies to keep people safe while protecting their privacy and sensory rights.
STEVE MANN AND CHRISTINA MANN

Prostheses for kids must match their condition and stage of development. Teams of scientists, engineers, designers, doctors and others work together to get them right.

FATCAMERA/GETTY IMAGES

HELPING PEOPLE WITH DISABILITIES

People with disabilities are often the first to use wearables, and doing so helps researchers understand how humans and machines can best work together.

Using Bionic Limbs to Climb Mountains

As a kid Hugh Herr was a star rock climber. He scaled mountains that adults hadn't attempted. Then tragedy struck. As a teenager he became trapped in a blizzard on a difficult ice route. Luckily, he was rescued, but he had frostbite on his legs. They had to be amputated below the knees. Herr wondered if he'd ever climb again.

But in less than a year, Herr created prosthetic legs for himself with the help of a prosthetist. He went on to become an engineer and biophysicist—and a creator of bionic limbs.

Herr is now one of the world's leading innovators and a star climber. "I climb at a more advanced level with my artificial limbs," he says.

Climbers, dancers and soldiers have written to him about their illnesses or injuries. They're hoping Herr can fix them. And he's trying. But the designs cost tens of thousands of dollars. So he's working with insurance companies to see if they'll pay for the prototypes.

Herr imagines a future in which technology eliminates disability for people. "It's like a magic fairy granted your wish," he says. "People ask me if I'd want my biological legs back if I could have them. No way! My bionic legs are part of my body—physically, psychologically and emotionally." Herr says he might get old, but his legs will still be strong. He can always get replacement parts. "It's like they're immortal," he says.

"Nothing can hold me back! I have state-of-the-art prosthetic limbs."

SOLSTOCK/GETTY IMAGES

MOVE SLOW + THINK HUMAN

People See Disability Differently

"I'm happy the way I am. I'm not impaired. I'm a variation," says Gregor Wolbring, a biochemist at the University of Calgary. Wolbring was born without legs. "Humans are better off if they accept imperfection," he says. If we're always striving for perfection, it could lead to a race to enhance abilities.

Not everyone with a disability wants to be "fixed" with technology. "People see disability as a personal tragedy—it's not," says Patty Berne. She's an advocate for disability justice and says many people just want a working wheelchair and not to be poor. "I use a wheelchair," says Berne. "It's an amazing machine."

She says there's a rush to spend billions on augmenting people with technology while their basic needs are forgotten. People first want healthcare, jobs and accessible places to live and go.

Building Our Strength with Wearable Robots

Exoskeletons are like wearable robot suits. They apply robotics, mechanics and electronics to provide people with extra strength and endurance. For example, soldiers, firefighters and factory workers can wear an exoskeleton to help them carry heavy loads or cross rugged terrain. People who have difficulty walking because of illnesses or injuries can wear them to help walk or climb stairs.

Exoskeletons help people with physically limiting illnesses or injuries to walk.
NICOLA TREE/GETTY IMAGES

When Manmeet Maggu was an engineering student at university, he became fascinated with robotics. At the same time, his family learned that his nephew Praneit had cerebral palsy. It's a disorder that affects a person's muscle tone, movement and motor skills. And it can affect each person differently. Praneit couldn't sit, stand or walk on his own.

Maggu did some research and learned it's not healthy for children to sit in a wheelchair all day. They need physical activity. He searched for a solution. There were exoskeletons for adults, but nothing for kids.

Maggu and his friend Rahul Udasi decided to use their robotics skills to help. They designed many prototypes. Finally they created the Trexo Plus. It's a pair of robotic legs that attach to a child's legs. The legs are used with a walker.

"What happened next was amazing," says Maggu. "My nephew could stand and walk on his own for the first time in his life." Every time Praneit's legs moved, he smiled. Maggu said Praneit felt confidence and pride. He could do something that wasn't possible before.

Now Trexo Robotics is helping kids across North America. Maggu hears hundreds of incredible stories of kids learning to ride a bike or walking up stairs for the first time. "We're not building robots," says Maggu. "What we're building is the magic when you see your child take their first steps."

Maggu and Udasi work closely with kids, their families and physiotherapists to make sure the Trexo is safe and comfortable. Many features, like angles, force and speed, are adjustable to make sure it's always helping the child as they grow. Maggu's vision is to make the Trexo available for every child who wants one. And they're looking for ways to help families pay for it.

But not all kids who can't walk want them. Some like their wheelchairs. "It's important to realize that," says Maggu. Some kids feel super cool with the robotic legs, like an Iron Man, but others don't.

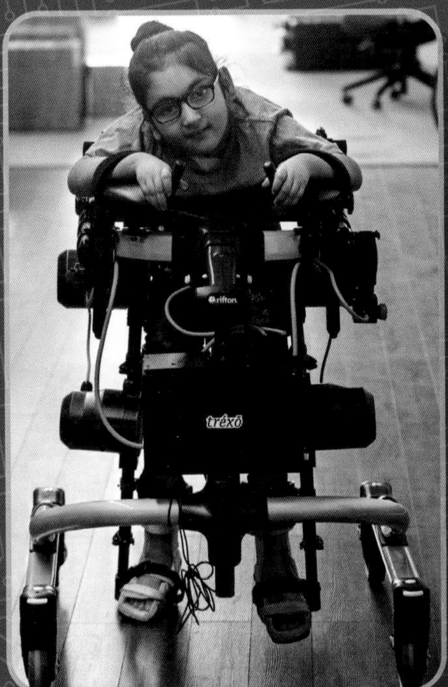

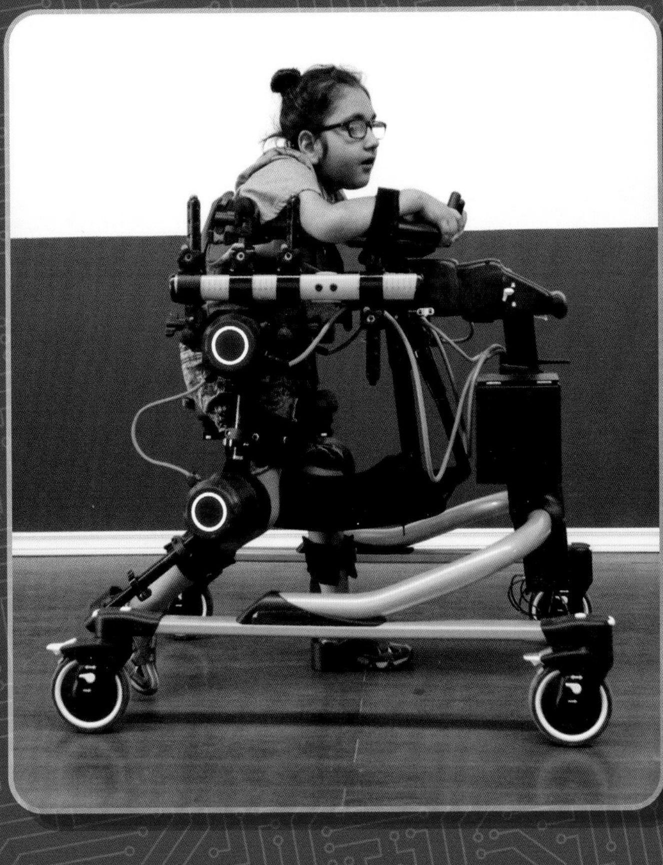

Praneit's excited to walk for the first time in his life. The Trexo team believes walking is a basic mobility right and that their device can help kids become active and empowered.

MANMEET MAGGU/TREXO ROBOTICS

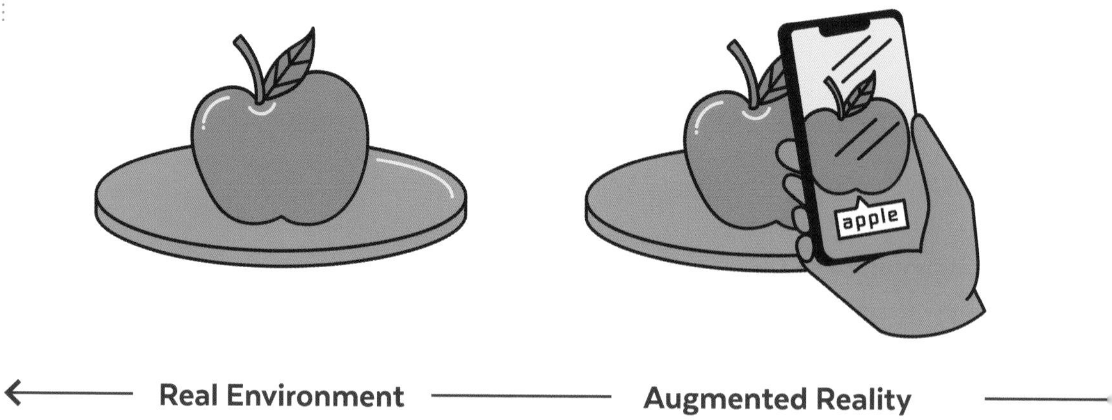

Nintendo released the mobile AR game *Pokémon Go* in 2016, and it became one of the most downloaded games in history.

KEONGDAGREAT/SHUTTERSTOCK.COM

SHAPING OUR EXPERIENCES WITH IMMERSIVE TECHNOLOGIES

Meet the immersive technology cousins: augmented reality (AR), mixed reality (MR) and virtual reality (VR). According to experts, immersive technologies will be the next major game changer for our world. The internet and smartphone were the last two big ones.

What Is Augmented Reality?

AR technology allows you to layer digital (virtual) images, sounds, videos, text or graphics on top of the real world. AR expands (augments) reality—it doesn't replace it. A person could experience AR by wearing a headset (head-mounted device), smart glasses or contact lenses, or using handheld devices like smartphones or iPads.

There are endless examples of smartphone-driven AR apps. One fun app is Nintendo's game *Pokémon GO*. Players hunt on their smartphone or tablet for virtual creatures scattered in public spaces. For some people, the game's

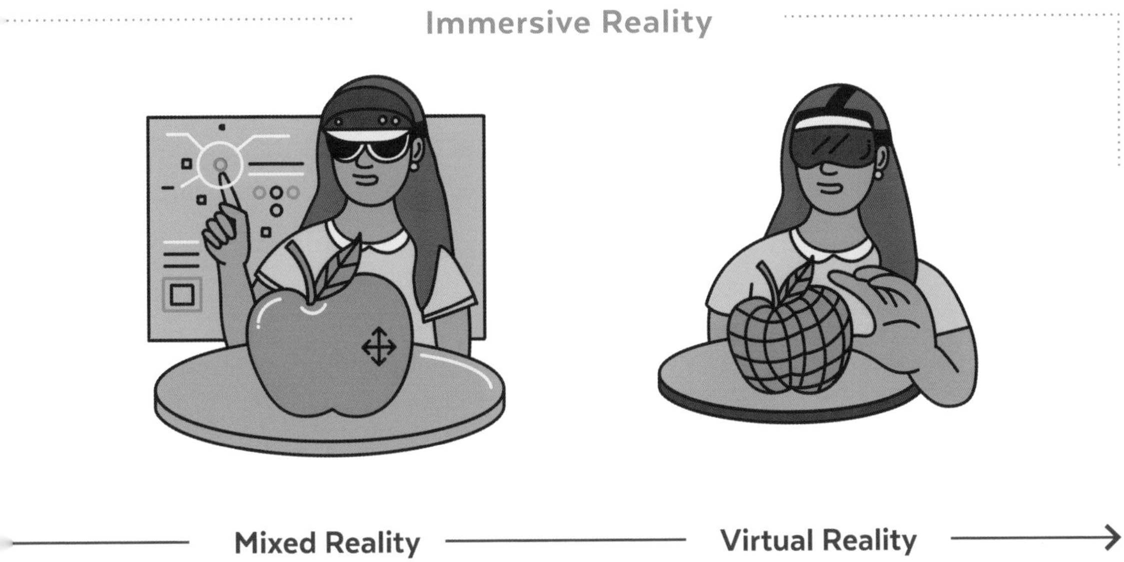

design is so immersive that they end up bumping into things. Safety first! Nintendo says you need to stay aware of your surroundings.

Beyond gaming, there are many AR applications for tourism, education, retail, training, healthcare and the military. Imagine that you're visiting a new city. You wear AR-capable smart glasses or contact lenses on a guided tour. As you look at buildings, descriptions appear in the visual display.

Smart AR glasses can enrich our lives with information.
SASIN PARAKSA/SHUTTERSTOCK.COM

Every millisecond matters in MR. The headsets must instantly capture what's happening in the real world, process it, render it and then display it.
KHOAMARTIN/DREAMSTIME.COM

What Is Mixed Reality?

MR technology is like AR in that virtual information is placed on top of the real world. But MR goes one step further. It allows users to work with virtual objects that are placed in the real world as if they were actual objects.

To experience MR, a person wears a wireless head-mounted device. Microsoft's HoloLens is a popular example. This device uses sensors, advanced optics and holograms. Suddenly you can see 3D objects floating in midair or virtual screens on a wall. You still see the real world in front of you, and you can walk around and talk to people without bumping into things.

Holograms display information that can blend with the real world or simulate a virtual world. There are many applications in education, training, sports, medicine, engineering and construction. For example, if you're an engineer, you could have a hologram of an engine you've designed. Then you can interact with the design. You can make it bigger or smaller, move around it and play with it to improve it. You can work with the engine the same way you would in the real world.

This engineer is placing a virtual robotic arm on a production line to study how it works and make sure it operates safely and efficiently.
WITTHAYA PRASONGSIN/GETTY IMAGES

What Is Virtual Reality?

When you're absorbed in something, it's called immersion. If you think about it, you can become immersed in a book, movie or video game and feel like you're lost in another world. But VR is different.

The real world is shut out. You're totally immersed in an interactive, computer-generated world you believe is real. As you move, the detailed 360-degree VR world moves with you. Your senses are fooled because of what VR experts call ***psychological presence***.

Three main features make "presence" and the feeling of "being there" possible. They are tracking, rendering and display, says Jeremy Bailenson. He's a VR expert at Stanford University's Virtual Human Interaction Lab.

Strap on a VR headset. Edge out onto a virtual plank and look down 80 stories. Some people gasp. Others fall and cry in fear. Richie's Plank Experience shows the power of "presence," says Jeremy Bailenson. "The feeling's *too* real."

TOAST VR PTY LTD., PROUD MAKERS OF RICHIE'S PLANK EXPERIENCE

A tracking system with cameras, gyroscopes and other sensors captures and measures a person's head and body movements. Rendering takes these movements and creates 3D models representing the sights, sounds, smells and touches for newly tracked locations. And for every tracked action, the digital information in the scene must be rendered for the new location. The display is the way digital images reach our eyes.

You can wear a headset (head-mounted display) or be in a cave automated virtual experience (CAVE) to experience VR. A CAVE is a room with screens that cover the walls, ceiling and floor. Images are projected onto the screens. Either way, you move around immersed in a 360-degree virtual (computer-generated) 3D world.

Use VR to up your tennis game!
ANNA SADOVSKAIA/SHUTTERSTOCK.COM

If you use ***haptic*** devices like data gloves or a wand, you can feel other people or objects in the environment. There's audio through headphones or surround sound. And you experience sights, sounds, touch and sometimes scent through the technology.

You'll find VR applications for things such as training, education, science, medicine, design and entertainment. And researchers are exploring ways to use VR to learn about how different people perceive and experience the world.

VR Improves Training

"VR is the ultimate training machine," says Bailenson. He says it helps you become better at mental and physical tasks because you're actually doing the things you would do in the real world. The military has been using VR for decades to help soldiers train. Pilots, sports teams and doctors use it too. Even businesses are using VR to train employees. It can help people working in stores or banks learn how to react to unexpected situations like armed robbery.

VR's an incredible training tool because you can practice and repeat tasks in simulated but real situations, anywhere, anytime. Athletes can work on mental repetitions or try out different game scenarios without the wear and tear on their bodies. Surgeons can practice new procedures and train medical students without risks to patients. Pilots can safely test different landing maneuvers. You can practice dangerous actions and learn from your mistakes without harming yourself or others.

VR Turns Kids into Scientists

Imagine using VR to learn what it's like to be a scientist. Chris Dede at Harvard University created EcoMUVE, a project for teaching kids about ecosystems. A MUVE, or multiuser virtual environment, is a 3D virtual world that

TECH_BYTE

VR's Not for All Learning

"We can't just shove all learning into VR goggles," says VR expert Jeremy Bailenson. For some things, textbooks or videos work better. But VR's great when you have to look around, move around or repeat physical tasks. Hike Mount Everest to study weather patterns, for example. Transport yourself back in time to experience history. Travel to the moon. VR makes amazing field trips possible. But it's important to find the right experience for VR.

looks and feels like a video game. In EcoMUVE students move around as avatars. They talk to other avatars and run experiments in detailed environments.

Students can explore freshwater ponds to learn about organisms in their natural habitats. They can walk in the water or use a micro-submarine to zoom in to observe. They can collect water measurements and visit the pond over a number of virtual "days" to observe changes with seasons. In the next level, students can explore a hardwood forest ecosystem over 50 virtual "years" to observe changes in animal populations and vegetation. Dede proved that even kids who have a tough time with science love it because VR makes learning meaningful and fun.

> **TECH_BYTE**
>
> **VR and Kids' Brains**
>
> Kids' brains are still developing, and researchers are learning that kids who use VR can become more confused than adults about what's real and what's virtual. They can develop false memories, which means they "remember" things that didn't happen in real life. Because VR experiences are so rich in detail, the brain confuses VR and the real world. Plus, they experience VR so intensely it can cause aggression or addiction. It can become hard to resist temptations or leave the virtual world. Most manufacturers have warnings. *Not for kids under 13. May cause dizziness. Don't use for more than five minutes.* What would you do if you saw these words?

VR Can Make New Experiences Feel Safe

Visiting the dentist can cause anxiety for some kids. So can riding a bus to school or camp. This is especially true for kids with autism, says Azadeh Kushki. She and her research team at the Holland Bloorview Kids Rehabilitation Hospital in Toronto are conducting studies to see if VR can help reduce kids' anxiety by exposing them to an experience in a safe and controlled way. It's called exposure therapy. So far the results are promising!

Kids use the school-bus VR headset for only five minutes. For the dental visit, kids take home a tablet loaded with the experience. For between 5 and 15 minutes a day over a week, they can feel what it's like to sit in the chair or have their teeth cleaned, in a 360-degree video experience.

"With all applications, we guard against VR side effects like headaches or dizziness or kids mixing up real and virtual worlds," says Kushki. These things can happen when you use VR for long periods. VR has a lot of potential, but she says it's important to use it carefully.

Robin is testing the VR headset for the robot. The robot captures still images or videos from home, using a 360-degree camera, and sends them to space for the astronauts to view in VR.
JUSTIN GREAVES/METROLAND

VR for Astronauts? Young Inventors Reduce Loneliness

Meet the Guardians of the Galaxsee! The team won first place at the *FIRST* LEGO League 2018–2019 international robotics competition. (*FIRST* means "for inspiration and recognition of science and technology"). At the time, the Guardians were eighth-grade students at Glen Ames Senior Public School in Toronto.

They designed a VR application to help astronauts with loneliness in space. It's called Home Away from Home. A robot with a 360-degree camera records memorable events in the astronauts' homes, such as their kids' birthday parties. The videos are sent to the astronauts to watch in VR. This allows them to experience those family events and stay connected. It helps with the astronauts' mental health, as space missions are long and lonely.

Adam and Tommy are discussing the 360-degree camera that's used with the robot. The camera brings images of familiar faces and places right to the astronaut.
JUSTIN GREAVES/METROLAND

"One of the coolest things about it is that the application can be used in other ways too," says team member Grace. "There are lots of reasons that families can't be together in person. Like parents who work in the military or when kids are sick in the hospital. But with VR, they can share memories like they're together!"

This military dad is using VR technology to watch his family at home and stay connected to their lives.

TOP: MONKEY BUSINESS IMAGES/ SHUTTERSTOCK.COM

BOTTOM: REALPEOPLEGROUP/ GETTY IMAGES

VR's Cool, But...

Can VR promote climate-change awareness or teach empathy? Experts are studying these possibilities and much more. So far the results look promising.

But Bailenson is very clear—VR should not be used for everything. When does VR work best? Which applications are successful? When is it harmful? Researchers are still learning.

"There are no rules in a VR world," he says. "You can go back in time. You can be another person. You can walk through chairs." There are no physical or mental limitations. But he says the brain treats VR experiences as if they're real. "VR is super intense," says Bailenson. In any experience in VR, you feel emotions as you'd feel them in the real world. So be careful, he says. If you wouldn't want to have a certain experience in real life, you don't want to have it in VR.

IMPROVING LIFE IN REAL TIME

Are wearables getting smarter? "Yes!" says Joni Kettunen, CEO of Firstbeat Technologies. He spoke to a crowd at the annual Consumer Electronics Show in Las Vegas. Thousands of industry leaders flock to this event every year to discuss and launch the newest technologies. In 2020 wearables were the stars of the show.

Many improvements work together to boost wearables along their smart journeys. AI capabilities are exploding.

Sensors are becoming smaller and more precise. Innovations in software, ***materials science***, robotics, cloud computing, IoT and other technologies are soaring.

Students in Victoria, Australia, are learning all about it. Schools there have partnered with tech industries for hands-on education. In one project, they're working with motion-capture (mocap) technology to digitally record people's movements. Students slip into a mocap suit called the Xsens. They perform movements from sports they play and then analyze their movements. It's a new way to learn about sports science, how the human body works and technology.

Sensors embedded in clothing and straps collect data about a full range of body movements. Tiny motion trackers are able to capture the smallest twitches. AI technologies process the data and upload it to the cloud. Students can see their real-time body movements come to life on the school's ***smartboards***.

This actor wears a specialized mocap suit and head rig that digitally record his movements for animations or visual effects in movies. An example of a well-known film with lots of mocap technology is *Avatar*.

GORODENKOFF/SHUTTERSTOCK.COM

Mocap is the result of over 100 years of innovation and computational advances. Now students can wear suits with sensors and see their movements come to life on a screen.

GIPPSLAND TECH SCHOOL

Smartwatches can help build healthy habits. Turn on the fun and fitness!

GAHSOON/GETTY IMAGES

Smart rings use advanced sensor technology. They can detect health information such as heart rate, sleep patterns and even stress level. Using Bluetooth, they sync with your smartphone to deliver reports. They can control other smart devices too.

AITOR DIAGO/GETTY IMAGES

Smartwatches and Fitness Trackers

There are hundreds of brands with exercise tracking and health features. These sleek devices have personal-activity intelligence systems that help you set and reach goals. *You ran five miles! Get more sleep!* Some research shows that people who track their exercise are more likely to stick with their routines.

Swipe left! Smartwatches include many other features too. For example, you can connect to the internet to answer calls, texts and emails.

Smart Rings

Wearables for your fingers? Some people like rings instead of watches because they have similar features but are more comfortable. There's a lot of technology packed into these tiny devices. You can even use your smart ring to pay for things.

Smart Clothing Improves Muscle Performance

Devon Lewis started a company called Impulse that's developing AI-powered clothing for sports. Sensors in the clothing monitor muscle activity. They send the information to an AI tool within the clothing. It calculates what muscles need stimulating. Then electrical impulses are delivered to those muscles through a network of wires in the fabric. The impulses feel like a tingling sensation. They're not harmful, and the stimulation increases the strength of the muscles. There's also an app that processes the data from the clothing so wearers can track their performance and see muscle imbalances and improvements. People can see this info on their smartphones. It's like wearing a personal trainer!

Integrating technology into clothes for sports or everyday use might one day transform how we interact with our world. Smart pants, shirts, shoes...underwear?

Lose something? Apple's AirTag is a Bluetooth tracker that attaches to any personal item and pairs to your smartphone. If something's lost or stolen, you can activate Apple's Find My app and, using ultra-wideband technology, be pointed to the item's precise location.

INK DROP/SHUTTERSTOCK.COM

Can't Decide Which Powered Clothing to Buy?

Google's Project Jacquard took intelligent clothing to a new level. They developed a smart tag that slips into any piece of clothing or object.

They also partnered with Levi's to launch a jacket with built-in sensors and conductive fabric. You can answer calls, play music and take photos right from your sleeve.

Smart Glasses

Smart glasses have small computers that process information and display the results in real time. Only the wearer can see the information, which includes text messages, map directions, incoming phone calls, fitness statistics and more.

Some have brain-computer interfaces (BCIs). Others have wireless stereo sound with noise-canceling ability,

MOVE SLOW + THINK HUMAN

I Don't Consent!

While smart glasses may be great for the person wearing them, what about the people around them? Since the glasses are always on, data on other people may be unintentionally tracked and recorded, and that information could be shared without their knowledge.

Your eyes can have superpowers! Smart contact lenses improve your vision. They also have built-in displays to enrich your daily life with timely information about the world around you.

HQUALITY/SHUTTERSTOCK.COM

built-in microphones or cameras. Many have AR and VR technology, even video streaming. And they're prescription-ready to help you see too.

Designers and engineers are working on smart glasses that look and feel like regular glasses. As they become less clunky and more stylish, they'll become more popular.

Smart Contact Lenses

Bionic eyes are here! Smart contact lenses were invented by Steve Mann in the 1990s. These days, they have many applications. Some are for medically treating eye diseases. Others are for correcting vision. But here's the cool bionic part—AR contact lenses with built-in visual displays. A company called Mojo Vision is bringing them to market. Look at the sky and learn about the galaxies. Look at maps while you're walking. You can see all these things without looking at a screen or holding a device.

MOVE SLOW + THINK HUMAN

Wearables Collect Tons of Personal Information

"Everything on the planet can be hacked," says computer scientist and author Ramez Naam, who teaches at Singularity University in California. "With the explosion of wearables, we're increasing the attack surface."

Immersive technologies collect data on our unique body movements. Connected smart devices collect location, heart rate, voice sounds and other information. Companies are building our profiles. They can track and target us with ads or worse. They can use and sell your info without your knowledge or consent. And who knows how secure their systems are? Hackers could get in and steal your identity. Developers are often quick to release the latest cool gadget, and they don't think protecting your privacy and security is a priority. What data do your devices collect?

Smart Hearables

Smart hearables are microcomputers that fit in your ear canal. Is there too much information coming at you? Smart hearables can detect this and take action. For example, if you can't hear your friend speaking over loud music, the hearable will automatically amplify your friend's voice.

Incredibly, smart hearables can also help monitor your health. Sensors positioned in the ear will track heart rate more reliably than wrist devices. ***Microelectrodes*** will track brain waves better than current methods on the scalp. Researchers say that tomorrow's smart hearables will combine ***physiological data*** and AI to diagnose and treat heart problems, depression, epilepsy and other conditions.

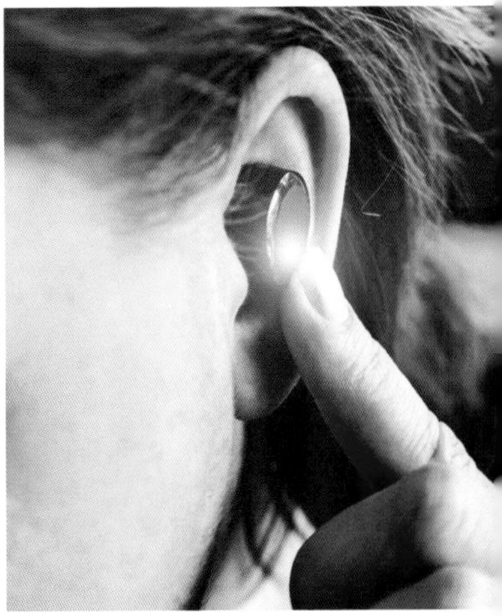

Smart hearable technology is developing fast and becoming popular.
MIKKELWILLIAM/GETTY IMAGES

Three

We're Augmenting Our Humanness

Technologies aren't just changing our lives—they're changing us! News flash! "The next decade will be the Age of Experience," declared Hyun-Suk Kim at the 2020 Consumer Electronics Show in Las Vegas. Kim is the president and CEO of Samsung Electronics. He talked about how smart wearables, homes, cars and cities will be designed to understand us as individuals. "Intelligent devices will predict our desires and react to our needs," he says.

Attendees say the Consumer Electronics Show is the most influential tech event in the world.

KOBBY DAGAN/SHUTTERSTOCK.COM

Super strength. Super hearing. Super vision. Super expression. Super connection. Super intelligence. Super experiences. People are on a quest to make humans better. Why shouldn't we upgrade the human body? How can our devices help us live even better lives? Let's create Humans 2.0!

Challenge accepted! Researchers and technologists are learning how to make wearables smaller, faster, more precise and more user-friendly. They're making them smarter too, with the intelligence to understand us and execute tasks on their own. They no longer need our commands. And we're able to connect to these devices through our brains, skin, eyes, ears and other body parts.

But something else is happening too. Our minds and bodies are melding with our devices. It's called ***human-machine symbiosis***. And it's about humans and computers becoming part of one another to boost human performance. We're collaborating as teammates!

Human-machine symbiosis is a vision that began in the 1960s. Now it's a reality.

MOVE SLOW + THINK HUMAN

Just Because We Can, Should We?

Just because we can meld our minds and bodies with machines, should we? After all, we don't know much about how this will affect us in the long term. The benefits can be exciting. But how do we make sure everyone who wants or needs new technology can get it? And how do we make sure it's safe for those who will use it?

BRAIN-COMPUTER INTERFACES

Imagine being totally alert but not being able to walk, speak or move your hands to turn on a light switch. It's like you're locked in your body. Now imagine a technology that helps you do things using only your thoughts. That technology is called a *brain-computer interface* (BCI).

Researchers have been developing BCIs for decades to help people with brain injuries or spinal disorders. Sometimes people are born with complex disabilities that leave them unable to speak, walk or move at all. Sometimes accidents or illnesses cause these things.

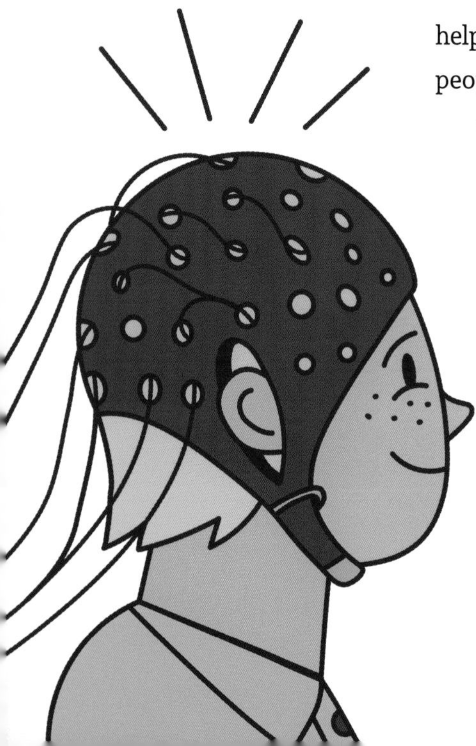

With BCIs, people can control their wheelchairs or operate prosthetic limbs with their thoughts. Or they can control things in their environment, like a virtual keyboard to play games or communicate. Researchers are exploring new ways to use BCIs. For example, they've been combining them with other technologies, such as virtual reality (VR) and augmented reality (AR), for education, training and mental-health therapy. They're also experimenting with brain-to-brain communication.

That's right! Maybe one day people will be able to connect with one another's brains using technology.

What Is a BCI?

A BCI is a technology that allows a direct communication link between a person's brain and external technology so that they can control that technology. A BCI detects the electrical and/or biochemical signals in the brain. A computer program reads and processes the signals using machine learning algorithms. Then the computer does the task the user imagines by connecting with nearby technology, such as a robotic arm or a virtual keyboard.

BCIs open up a world of communication possibilities.

ADAPTED FROM "BRAIN-COMPUTER INTERFACES FOR CHILDREN WITH COMPLEX COMMUNICATION NEEDS AND LIMITED MOBILITY: A SYSTEMATIC REVIEW," © ORLANDI, HOUSE, KARLSSON, SAAB AND CHAU, *FRONT. HUM. NEUROSCI*, JULY 14, 2021. DOI.ORG/10.3389/FNHUM.2021.643294

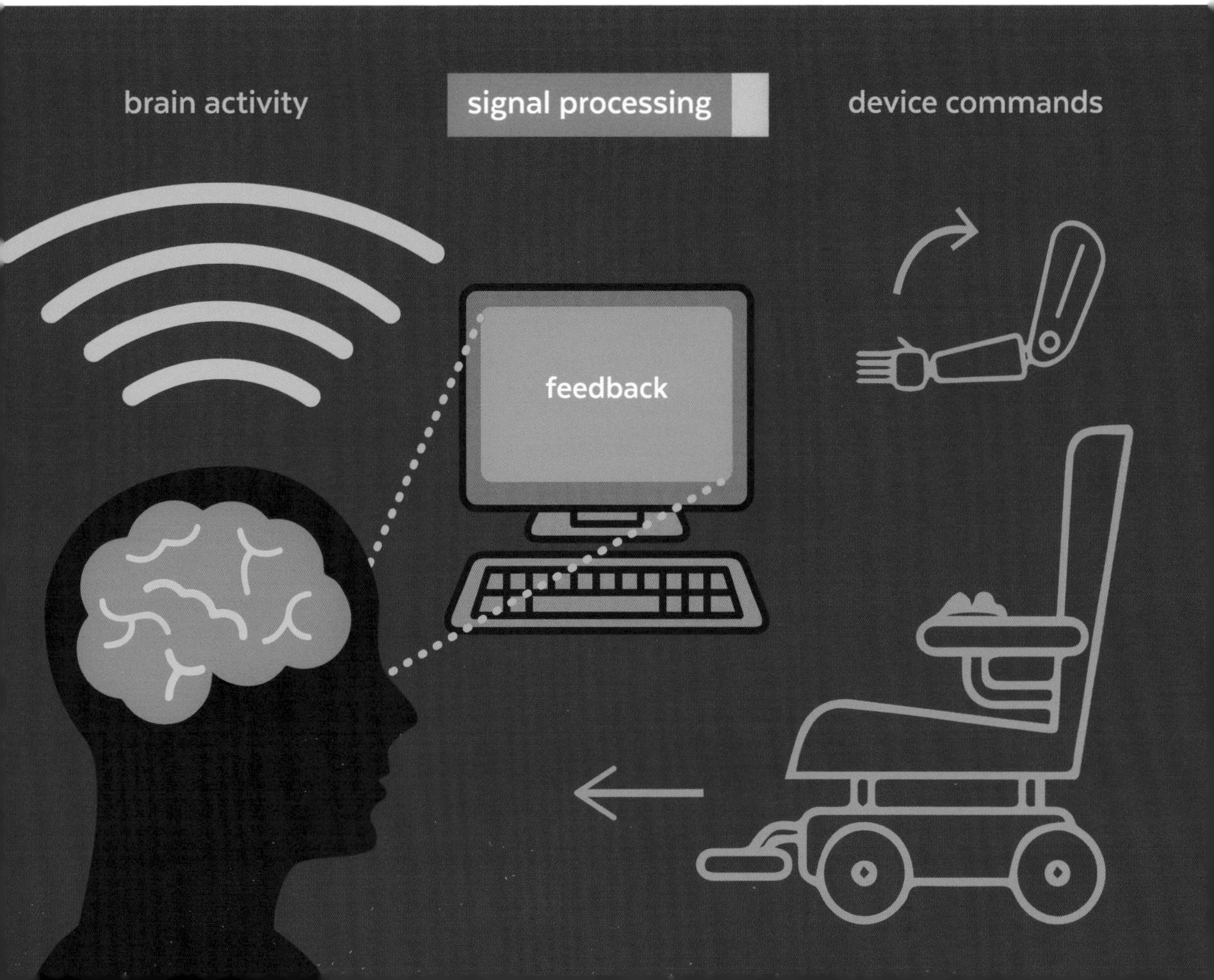

BCIs detect brain signals in several ways. They can detect them from inside the brain with implanted micro-electrodes. Another way is recording from the brain's surface, inside the skull. But surgery's not always practical or the right approach. There are also two head-cap methods for detecting signals from outside the scalp using sensing electrodes. The first is called *electroencephalography*, or *EEG* for short. This technology measures the electrical activity of neurons (nerve cells) in the brain. The other is called ***functional near-infrared spectroscopy***. It uses a special type of light to detect brain signals by measuring changes in blood flow and oxygen levels.

What about BCIs for Kids?

BCIs are state-of-the-art wearable technology, but until recently they were just for adults. Tom Chau is the vice president of research at the Holland Bloorview Kids Rehabilitation Hospital in Toronto. He says they have switch-operated toys and video games connected to BCIs, and kids at the hospital can control them with their thoughts. "You should see their excitement," says Chau. If you've grown up having all your abilities, he says, it's impossible to know what it's like not to be able to control things in your environment.

The first time Brody used BCI technology, it was emotional for him and his mom because he could finally control something without anyone's help. Incredible!
DANA GEALL

Brody was born with nonverbal cerebral palsy. That means his muscles and motor skills are affected, and he can't speak. But Brody can play computer games with his thoughts. Brody loves playing a game where aliens cross the computer screen. When his target hovers over the alien, Brody has to think of hitting the alien at the perfect time. *Got 'em!* Way to go, Brody!

Chau says it's a basic human right to be able to communicate, so his team adopted the United Nations' Convention on the Rights of Persons with Disabilities. "These kids are smart, capable and they know what's going on around them," he says. "We believe it's our fundamental obligation to help them."

Put On the "Magic Hat"

What about a BCI that improves kids' self-esteem? Researchers Pattie Maes, Nataliya Kosmyna, Cassandra Scheirer, and Alexandra Gross at the Massachusetts Institute of Technology (MIT) Media Lab are showing that this is possible. What people think about themselves influences their self-esteem, say the researchers, so they built a Thinking Cap modeled on the sorting hat in the Harry Potter books. The "magic hat" system uses a state-of-the-art BCI and a Bluetooth speaker. When students wear the hat as they do math, it praises them for effort and ability. After testing the hat with 50 kids ages 8 to 12, the researchers found that students were eager to do math, and it had changed their beliefs about their abilities. Researchers say early results are promising. If the hat tells kids they're capable, they believe it!

And now there's Thinking Cap 2.0. It's a wearable system in the form of masks, tiaras or helmets from sci-fi universes like *Star Wars* or *Avengers*.

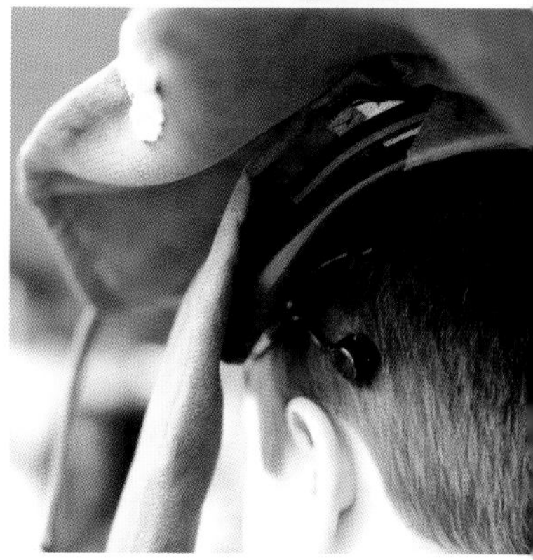

An EEG-based BCI (headset) and Bluetooth speakers fit in the Thinking Cap. The EEG captures the child's brain activity, then uses machine learning algorithms to help them study or complete tasks by praising their hard work.

TOP: JUDITH SIRERA I PULIDO

BOTTOM: NATALIYA KOSMYNA

TECH_BYTE

BCIs Are a New Skill for Humanity

Thinking a thought to move an object is a new skill for humanity. "BCIs are a new way to interface with the world," says Tom Chau. Our brains change when we learn any new skill, like playing the piano or drawing, and he says we don't know how BCIs will change our brains over the long term. That's especially true for kids because their brains are still developing. But BCIs open up a world of helping possibilities.

Soumiya envisions a world in which mental illness—an extremely personal struggle—is solved in equally personal ways!
SOUMIYA SIVASATHIYANATHAN

BCIs for Depression? Young Inventor Shoots for the Moon!

"I want to make a difference in the world," says Soumiya Sivasathiyanathan. She's had a passion for healthcare since she was a kid. Soumiya used to think studying medicine was the only way. Then she applied to The Knowledge Society's science, technology, engineering and mathematics (STEM) program for students ages 13 to 17. The goal of the society is to help students learn how emerging technologies can solve big world problems.

Students pick a problem that's important to them. Soumiya was concerned about the millions of people worldwide who suffer from depression. The illness can be caused by imbalances of chemical messengers in the brain. But people's brains are different, so the same medicines don't work for everyone. Sometimes the medicines don't work at all. She learned that BCIs might help.

Soumiya got busy on a moonshot project. Moonshot thinking is when you choose an impossibly huge problem and develop a radical idea to solve it using science and technology. It's about having the courage to try. Many great inventions happen this way.

Soumiya studied BCIs. She learned about an EEG-powered brain-sensing headband that can measure the brain's electrical activity. Soumiya asked herself, What if a headband like this had sensors that could measure the levels of the brain's chemical messengers?

She created a mock-up to test ideas. What if the headband could transmit levels to an app on a smartphone using Bluetooth? Then what if a machine learning algorithm in the app could determine if the messengers are off-balance and how much correction is needed? Maybe it would also be possible for electrodes in the band to deliver a gentle, mild current to special areas in the brain to restore balance.

Can we design a brain-sensing headband to detect and treat depression? I'm hopeful, says Soumiya. But it will take more research. Then it has to be available and affordable for everyone, even in the poorest corners of the world.

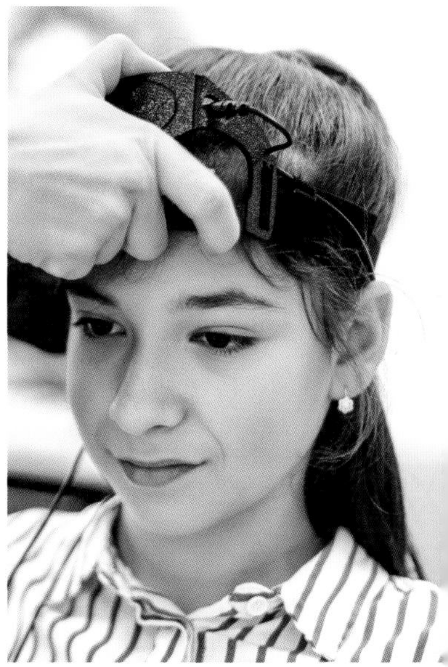

This young girl is working with a therapist to learn how to concentrate better.

ABO PHOTOGRAPHY/SHUTTERSTOCK.COM

BCIs Beyond the Medical World

What about BCIs for healthy people? There are many ways they're being used. Let's say you're having trouble focusing in class. You can work with a mental-health professional who reads your brain activity while you're wearing an EEG headset and playing a video game. If you remain focused, you receive a "reward" like a sound or a change in the image in the video. BCIs can help train your brain to focus, meditate and relax. Neuromarketing's getting more attention because businesses can use BCIs to see how customers react to their products in real time. And experimental military projects use BCIs so pilots can control aircraft and drones.

BCI technology is advancing, which makes it easier to use. But will BCIs replace other ***interfaces*** in our daily lives like keyboards, mice or remotes? Maybe, one day.

Brendan Allison is senior scientist at the University of California, San Diego. He says BCIs will have to become more practical, attractive, efficient and less expensive before they

How do you feel about products? Companies want to know so that you'll buy theirs! Neuromarketing is a blend of marketing and neuroscience. BCIs are used as a tool to understand consumers' emotional states when viewing different products.

MCLITTLE STOCK/SHUTTERSTOCK.COM

go mainstream. After all, who's going to have brain surgery voluntarily? And who wants to walk around with electrodes strapped to their head? Plus, learning to use BCIs takes time and skill, as the special mental tasks require concentration and practice.

But the bigger question for Allison is whether they're being developed safely and ethically. The medical world's standards are higher than industry's. He and other scientists are worried about the public's safety because they're seeing companies sell unregulated BCIs to consumers. Many don't work. Some make false claims. No, you can't read your pet's mind! And Allison says companies often don't want to pay for ethics training or product reviews and approvals.

But there's more. Harmful products are ruining the reputation of honest scientists who are using BCIs to help people. They're giving BCIs themselves a bad reputation. Allison and others are working on guidelines for the safe development and ethical use of BCIs.

MOVE SLOW + THINK HUMAN

Brain Helping or Hacking?

Companies are researching how BCIs can read your brain activity and potentially even read your mind. Meta has teams of engineers building BCIs. And they're supporting scientists at universities. Decoding speech directly from the human brain will be possible. And at a company called Neuralink, entrepreneur Elon Musk is working toward melding AI with the human brain with a brain implant so people can be smarter.

Before BCIs become mainstream, people must understand what's possible and the precious data they'll be giving up, says futurist and tech adviser Bernard Marr. "Do we want AI to be able to decode our thoughts?" he says. "Do we want our data in the hands of for-profit companies? I know I don't!"

LAB-GROWN HUMAN ORGANS AND TISSUES: THE ULTIMATE WEARABLES

Dean Kamen is a world-renowned inventor and engineer. He has invented hundreds of devices. One that made him famous is the Segway, a personal motorized scooter. He's also famous for co-founding *FIRST*, the organization behind the Guardians of the Galaxsee team you read about in chapter 2. Kamen wants to inspire youth to pursue careers in science and technology. Now he's on a new mission.

"We need human organ factories," says Kamen. Wounded soldiers need body parts. And hundreds of thousands of people die yearly waiting for organ transplants. That's why he set up a new company called the Advanced Regenerative Manufacturing Institute (ARMI).

ARMI is made up of hospitals, research institutions and companies where experts in engineering, medicine, life science and computer science work together. Scientists have made incredible breakthroughs growing organs, Kamen says, but there's no way to mass-produce them. That's where ARMI comes in. Its experts plan to develop large-scale manufacturing for engineered tissues and organs. That means building factories and training a workforce. "We'll start with skin, bone and cartilage," he says. "They're much simpler organs. But we'll get to hearts, lungs, livers and kidneys too, and within our lifetime."

SKIN INTERFACES

And the "wrist" is history! Wearables are moving beyond the wrist. With skin interface technologies like smart tattoos and bandages, we can help athletes improve their training, monitor babies' health more accurately, heal wounds, prevent skin cancer, control the world from our bodies and more. This revolution is just getting started!

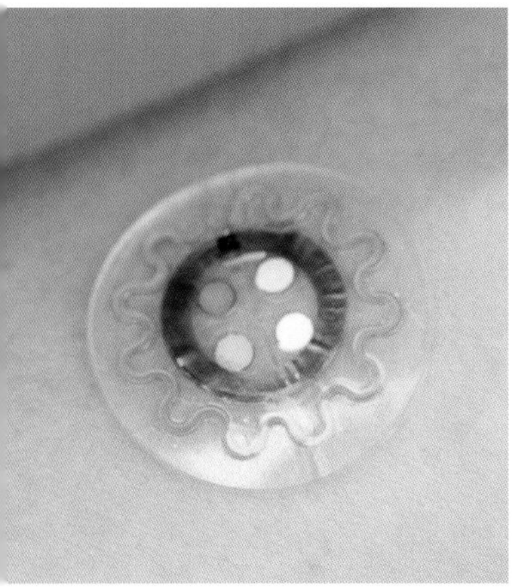

This microfluidic device is a little larger than a quarter and about the same thickness. It's low-cost and designed for one-time use.

JOHN A. ROGERS/NORTHWESTERN UNIVERSITY

Sweat Tells a Story

Dr. John Rogers and his team at Northwestern University developed the first-of-its-kind ***microfluidic*** device that captures and analyzes sweat and other fluids to show how a person's body is responding to exercise. It's like having a mini laboratory on your body! The soft, skin-like device wirelessly interfaces with a smartphone. The phone takes a picture and launches an app that indicates whether the wearer needs to drink more water or replenish salt or other minerals. This wearable electronic device can also monitor diseases in newborn babies and adults.

World's Smallest Wearable

It fits on your fingernail. This wearable sensor developed by Rogers and his team at Northwestern gives people information so they can develop healthy habits when they're in the sun. You swipe the device with your phone, and an app reports your exposure to ultraviolet (UV) radiation. The goal is to prevent sunburns and skin cancer. "It's always on," says Rogers. "And it weighs as much as a raindrop!"

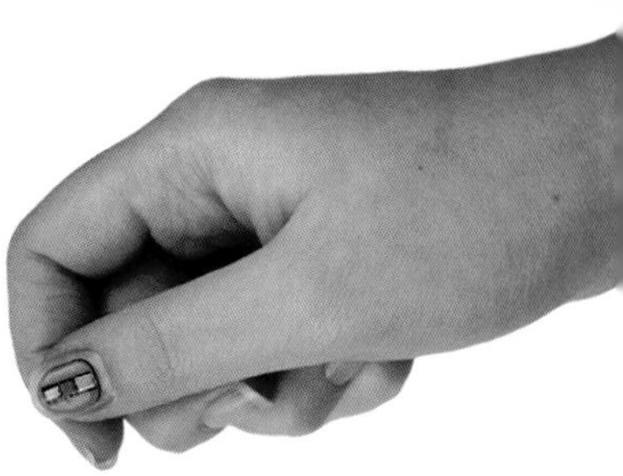

This tiny wearable can measure sun exposure more accurately than any other device on the market. And the design is customizable, so it fits on fingernails, clothing, jewelry and more.

JOHN A. ROGERS/NORTHWESTERN UNIVERSITY

Ping! "Your Wound Is Healing"

In 1920 Johnson & Johnson marketed the first Band-Aid—it's over 100 years old. Now engineers and scientists are reinventing a new generation of smart bandages. "Our new smart bandage can do the healing and thinking for you," says engineer Sameer Sonkusale. The smart bandage can track infection. Then it can deliver medicine to speed up healing. All through an app on your phone, you can know what's happening with your wound.

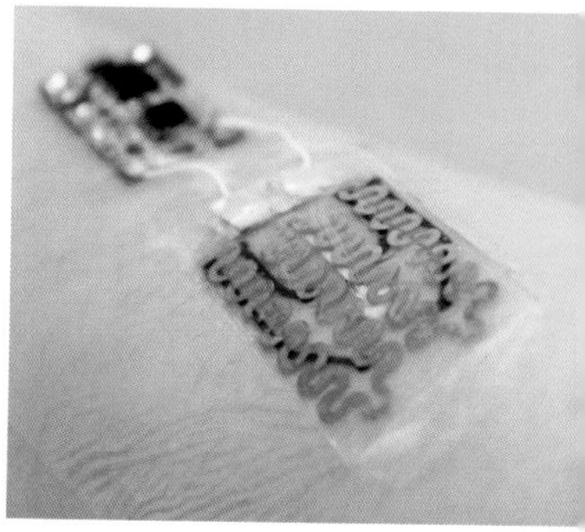

The smart bandage has many parts. One patch includes the sensors, microheater and drug carriers. A separate patch includes wireless electronics. Sameer Sonkusale says, "the biggest engineering obstacle was integrating all the different components into one bandage that stays flexible."

P. MOSTAFALU, S. SONKUSALE ET AL., TUFTS UNIVERSITY

Smart Tattoos Blend Art, Fashion, Science and Technology

Tattooing is an ancient practice that dates back more than 5,000 years. People have been using tattoos to mark an achievement or remember a special person or experience. Others use them simply for self-expression.

Today there's a new purpose for tattoos—they can be wearable electronic circuitry. Smart tattoos are interactive devices that enhance the function of your skin. Communicate with your smartphone. Pay for groceries. Monitor your heart rate. Researchers around the world are developing smart tattoos for many purposes. And they look cool too!

Teams at MIT Media Lab and Microsoft Research designed DuoSkin. They made it from gold- and silver-leaf materials. Users can control their mobile devices, display and store information, all while looking cool!

CINDY HSIN-LIU KAO & MIT MEDIA LAB

Left: Zap! You won't want to lie to someone if you're wearing the Holy Dress.
MELISSA COLEMAN

Right: Human flight is a reality with Richard Browning's Gravity Jet Suit. "To feel your feet lift off the ground, that ultimate freedom of true flight. This will be a day you remember for the rest of your life," says Browning.
THOMAS FAULL/GETTY IMAGES

FASHION + TECH = WAY MORE THAN A NEW LOOK

In 2020 the Museum of Science and Industry in Chicago hosted *Wired to Wear*, the first-ever exhibit on wearable technology. David Mosena is the museum's former president and CEO. He says they wanted the museum's visitors to understand why their closet will look totally different in only a few years. "Your wardrobe—and your life—will never be the same," he said.

A Dress That Shocks You When You're Lying?

Melissa Coleman is an artist and creative technologist. She specializes in fashion and tech. Coleman designed the Holy Dress. It's a wearable lie detector. It uses a voice sensor, copper conductors and warning lights. If the wearer tells a lie, it shocks them!

The Next Frontier in Human Flight

Richard Browning can fly, and you can too! He invented the Gravity Jet Suit. It has an exoskeleton and five small engines. It can travel more than 80 miles (129 kilometers) per hour.

Ever since Browning was a kid, he never stopped asking, "What if?" He grew up making model airplanes with his father, who was an aeronautical engineer. And as if exoskeletons weren't cool enough, Browning thought he'd design one for human flight.

"Engineering's the coolest career in the world," says Browning.

This limb is called Cuckoo. It's carved from cherrywood and features a working cuckoo clock, bell and pendulum. Sophie de Oliveira Barata made it for a dancer.

SOPHIE DE OLIVEIRA BARATA / ALTERNATIVE LIMB PROJECT. CARVED BY SAMUEL RUDMAN, ELECTRONICS BY RORY THOMPSON.

A Prosthetic Limb Just for You!

People have been fixing their bodies with technology for a long time. Now the field of prosthetics includes 3D printing, robotics, AI and BCIs to restore movement and touch sensation. People who have lost limbs through accidents or illness get their abilities back.

But why stop at function?

Sophie de Oliveira Barata understands that missing a part of your body can be traumatic. She talked to amputees and learned that prostheses can make your body feel whole again. But not everyone wants a limb that looks like a medical device, she says.

Barata is an artist trained in special-effects prosthetics. She creates personalized limbs. "Prosthetics can be a means of self-expression," she says. "They're like an extension of our personality."

That's why Barata created the Alternative Limb Project. She works with Paralympic athletes, music performers, models and even kids to design limbs tailored to them. Some limbs are covered in jewels. Others have stereos or secret compartments, or they're futuristic-looking. To build the limbs, Barata works with specialists in other fields, such as electronics and 3D modeling.

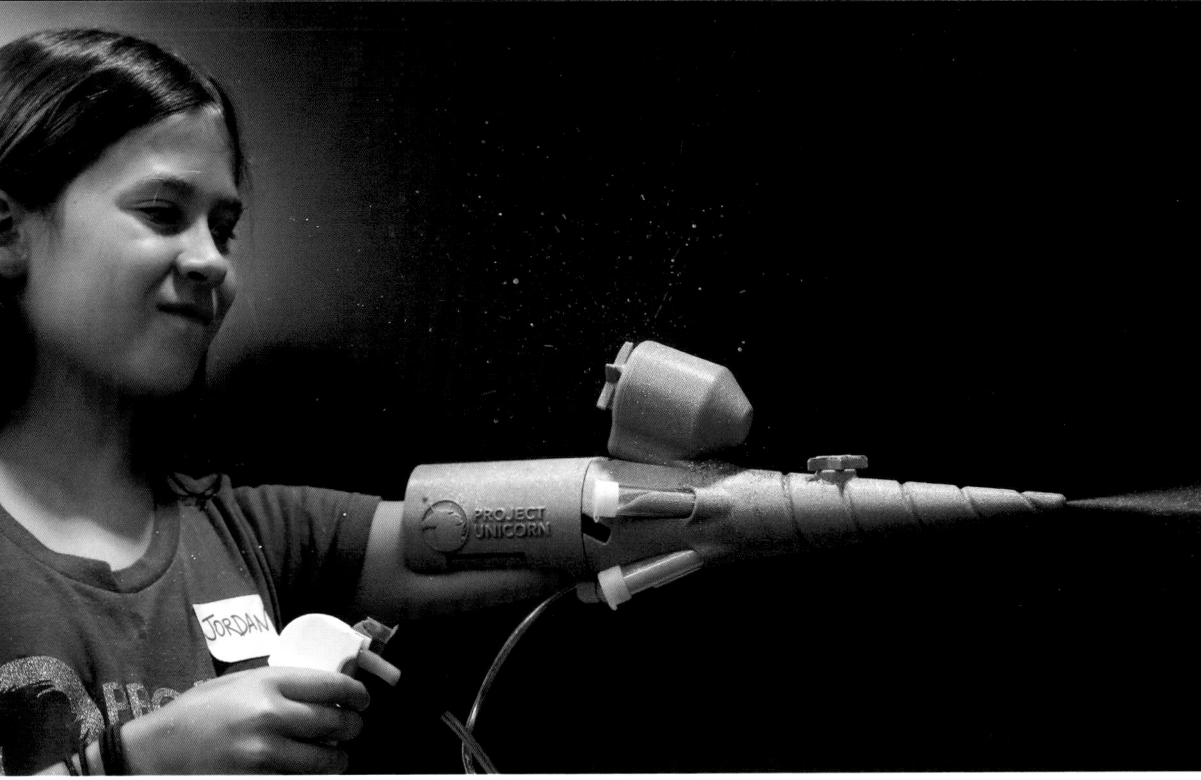

Jordan turned her disability into a superpower and then inspired kids to find creative solutions to their challenges. Jordan likes to think about her disability as a cool thing: "Someone with two hands can't shoot glitter out of their arm!"

PAT GREENHOUSE/THE BOSTON GLOBE/ GETTY IMAGES

Young Inventor Changing Kids' Lives

Jordan Reeves was born with a half left arm. Jordan uses prostheses to help her do things like ride a bike. When she was eight years old, she was invited to a camp for kids with limb differences. It was called Superhero Cyborgs. That's where she created Project Unicorn. It's a 3D-printed prosthetic arm that shoots glitter. "Kids with differences are like unicorns," says Jordan. "Not everyone acts or looks the same. But we're all perfect the way we are."

She says some people think having a disability is a bad thing, but it has created opportunities for her. Jordan is a mentor to other kids with disabilities. Her passion is spreading awareness about limb differences through science, technology, engineering, arts and mathematics (STEAM) education. Jordan and her mom formed an organization called Design With Us and wrote a book called *Born Just Right*. She has been featured on TV talk shows and TED Talks, and her famous limb is on display at design museums. She wants to help kids see that their differences give them perspective. They can see design flaws in products that people with a typical body can't see.

Jordan loves inventing and designing. One day she might want to be an industrial designer. "We need more people in the design community who are different," says Jordan. She's even an official superhero. Check out episode 1 of *Marvel's Hero Project* or read her book.

MOVE SLOW + THINK HUMAN

The Device Might Not Be Safe for You

There's a problem in tech development—devices aren't tested for safety and effectiveness on everyone. For example, when developers build new VR games, people who become sick or dizzy drop out of the study. That means the technology's made for people it already works for.

ARE WEARABLES GOOD TEAMMATES?

We can link our brains with devices that help us control our environment. We can wear clothes that protect us, or bodysuits that give us the power to fly. We can rely on sensors to warn us about sun danger. And we can choose prosthetic limbs that reflect our personalities. We are ***augmented*** humans working symbiotically with our devices. They're our teammates! But are they good teammates?

A smartwatch is helping this construction worker communicate quickly with other team members.
DUSANPETKOVIC/GETTY IMAGES

Four

Are We Crossing the Line?

LET'S TALK!

Wearable technology gives us superpowers to help and heal our bodies and minds. But is there a point where superpowers can become super problems?

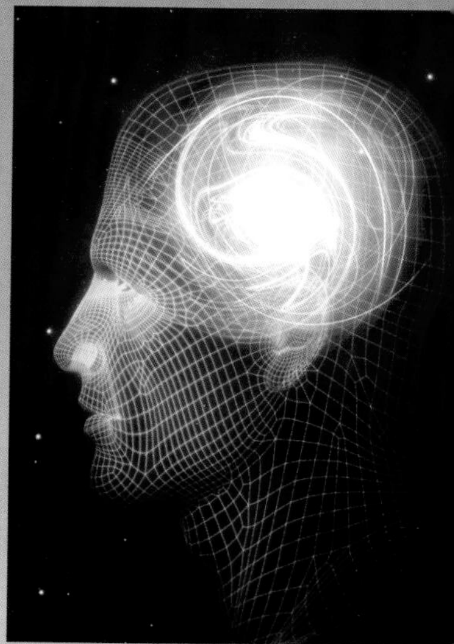

Brain scans allow scientists to observe how our brains use oxygen. By doing this, they can know things like what words someone is about to say, what images they're thinking of or what music they have in their head.
CHAD BAKER/GETTY IMAGES

"MIND-MELDING"—LET'S TALK ABOUT TELEPATHY

One day Mary Lou Jepsen had a *big* idea. I'm going to make a life-saving medical device, she thought. But...it will also make telepathy possible.

Jepsen's an electrical engineer and physicist in San Francisco. She started a company called Openwater. Along with her team, she invented a wearable medical imaging device. It can see deep inside your brain and show if there's a tumor. Her discovery is a huge deal for two reasons: it's life-saving, and one day it will be able to read your mind.

Right now hospitals use ***magnetic resonance imaging (MRI)*** machines to detect brain tumors. Tests are expensive, and two-thirds of people in the world can't afford them. Without an MRI test to confirm a diagnosis, people could die. Jepsen knows this firsthand. She almost died from a brain tumor because she couldn't afford an MRI. Then someone paid for her.

Openwater has taken this massive MRI machine that weighs about 4,000 pounds (about 1,800 kilograms), and shrunk it into a device that fits into a hat. It's a thousand times cheaper. And it gives doctors even better data to detect tumors and other diseases because the brain images have crisp, clear details.

But now Jepsen is speaking out about her project because she's also a little worried. With this technology she says we'll one day be able to "mind-meld." That means we'll be able to create a telepathic link to read one another's minds or exchange thoughts.

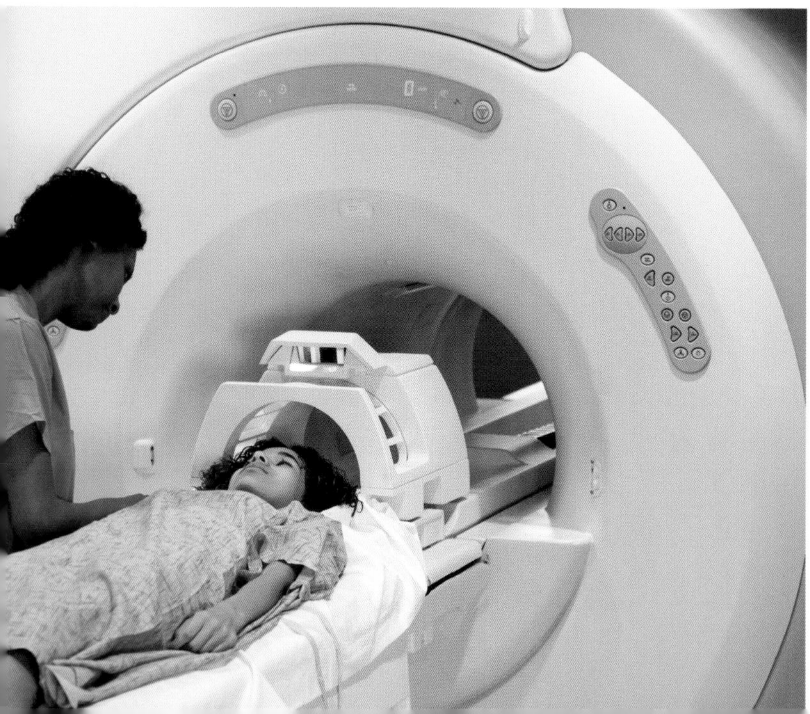

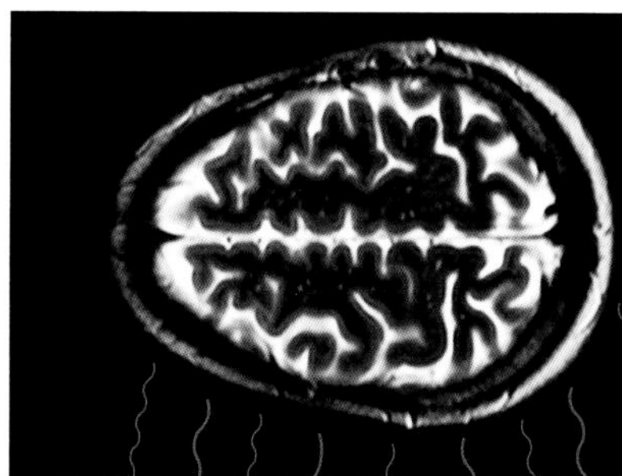

Openwater's groundbreaking research has shrunk massive MRI technology into a device that fits in a hat. Once approved by health authorities, this wearable MRI system will save millions of lives.

LEFT: ER PRODUCTIONS LIMITED/ GETTY IMAGES

RIGHT (TOP): PASIEKA/GETTY IMAGES

RIGHT (BOTTOM): MONKEYBUSINESSIMAGES/ GETTY IMAGES

Jepsen says we have to ask questions and make choices. Do we want to understand the brain? Do we want to save billions of lives? If we do, then we *will* have telepathy, because this technology will make it possible. "But there's no denying it, the ethics are huge," she says.

That's why she says that it's super important to have discussions *now* about how we'll use this technology. For example, can the military make you wear this technology? The police? Your parents?

"How will we protect people's data—their most private thoughts and feelings?" Jepsen asks. "What are the rules? We must talk about what it means to be responsible. Everyone should be part of the conversation."

TECH_BYTE

Transhumanists

Transhumanists believe that people who are perfectly healthy should be able to use science and technology to enhance their minds or bodies.

Remember Hugh Herr from chapter 2? He's the famous mountain climber and creator of bionic limbs. He says he's excited about technologies that will extend us physically, mentally and emotionally. "Anyways, what does it really mean to be human?" Herr asks. If he removed all four of his limbs and replaced them with bionic limbs, would he still be human? He thinks most people would say yes. "For me, to be human is what's happening in our brain and our heart."

Some people disagree. They worry it will lead to a race to enhance our abilities. What do you think? Are you a transhumanist?

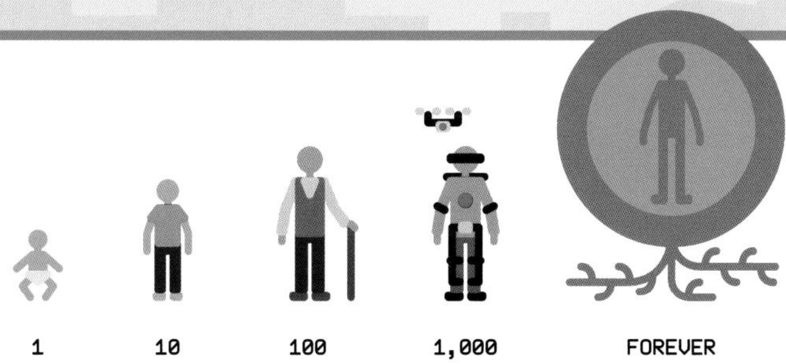

POTATOSAPIENS / SHUTTERSTOCK.COM

Can we prepare for living in a virtual world? When lifelike avatars move and sound like us, will this affect our ability to form authentic relationships? How will living in virtual bodies affect humanity over time?

RVLSOFT/SHUTTERSTOCK.COM

VIRTUAL BODIES—LET'S TALK ABOUT TELEPRESENCE

Being social in an online world isn't new. People often share experiences through gaming or just hanging out. They choose or create an avatar and meet up in simulated worlds using virtual reality (VR) systems. Creators are getting better at designing avatars that don't look cartoonlike, and our virtual bodies...they're about to get way more "real."

Companies, including Meta (formerly Facebook), Google and Apple, are working furiously to create lifelike avatars that are exact replicas of people. "They will be super-high-resolution models," says Michael Abrash. He's the chief scientist at Meta Reality Labs. He and other scientists are studying the human body to develop software that can read gestures and emotions. Social "presence," or the feeling of being there with a "real" person, is going to be possible in VR.

Connecting with others through phones and videos is okay, but it doesn't offer the same personal connection you get face-to-face. Being close, reacting to each other's body language and facial expressions—it's all part of a human experience that we need.

Remember VR expert Jeremy Bailenson from chapter 2? He says it's when people can talk, touch and hang out in a virtual space, and it feels like real life, that everyone will want VR. "But those of us designing social VR better get it right, and fast," he says. "This technology will transform our lives and the way we communicate."

Bailenson is optimistic. He believes we could fix many problems with social VR, including climate change. And we could improve our quality of life. We wouldn't waste hours commuting to work or school or traveling across the globe for meetings. We could reduce our use of gasoline and jet fuel. We'd save lives from car accidents, reduce the spread of diseases, save time and money. And we could meet friends and family anywhere, anytime. We could share any possible experience.

Imagine an avatar with the same funny smile, quirky walk or nervous tic your friend has. Together with photo-realistic 3D models and immersive audio, their looks and voice would be lifelike. And with haptic technology, even their hugs would feel real.

What's more, biometric tracking technologies would let us see things like readings of a person's heartbeat. You'd be

MOVE SLOW + THINK HUMAN

We Have Trust Issues

Remember Grace from Guardians of the Galaxsee in chapter 2? She says it's already hard enough to trust someone fully. When people are behind the computer screen, it's even harder. You really don't know who you're talking to especially when you can add filters like age or skin color. "They're only showing you what they want you to see," says Grace.

Grace is right! How will we be able to form trusting relationships with others as we live more parts of our lives in virtual worlds? And will we be able to trust our minds to know what's real and what isn't?

able to know if your friend was nervous even if they were trying to hide it. So you'd have more information about your friend in VR than if you were face-to-face.

Stop the Press!

These developments sound positive, but there are some downsides to consider. Won't avatars be super versions of us? If designers can create avatars without physical flaws, you can have a cuter smile or have a limp removed. And with newer versions of social VR, 3D models are stored on each person's machine. That means VR images are fixed. This is different from video technology. The camera sends everything it sees in video—every single pixel, in every single frame, is transmitted over the internet. These images aren't always flattering because they pick up imperfections. With fixed images, you can always look perfectly groomed in real time, even when you're not. But...who's the real you?

Let's go a step further. If we're designing our virtual bodies, why not choose a body that's a different gender, age or creature? Ingrid is a real-life professional game artist, and one of her avatars includes a "fish person" (half fish, half human). Then there's Oscar. He has been gaming for years, and his main avatar is a flying robot with a human brain. Oscar says he's shy in real life. But in social VR, he feels more like himself. Oscar prefers living in his virtual life.

According to researchers, people find new ways to express themselves and live their lives with social VR. For people with autism or other disabilities, having a different identity can be empowering and make the world feel safer. But what does it mean for society as a whole if people only interact virtually, through different digital identities?

MOVE SLOW + THINK HUMAN

Soon We May Not Recognize Humankind

Is there a human behind that VR headset? Gamers admit it's easy to forget real people are behind avatars when they can fly, teleport, change bodies, pass through "solid" objects or control the world with hand gestures and voice commands. If we live in social VR, what will that mean for identities? How will living in virtual and real worlds affect our brains?

MOVE SLOW + THINK HUMAN

Your Digital Bodyprint Is Not Safe

Let's imagine that a boy named Riley played a VR game for 20 minutes. While he was playing, the system recorded two million data points about his body movements. Then the game creators sold this data. Later, when Riley is trying to get life insurance, the company says no because Riley is at risk for a disease called Alzheimer's. But Riley is in good health. How could this happen?

VR systems collect data about our nonverbal behavior—body movements, eye gazes, facial expressions...everything. It can be used to predict and diagnose diseases. Health professionals would protect this data and use it to help Riley. But weak rules may mean industries can collect, use or share our data without our knowledge and consent.

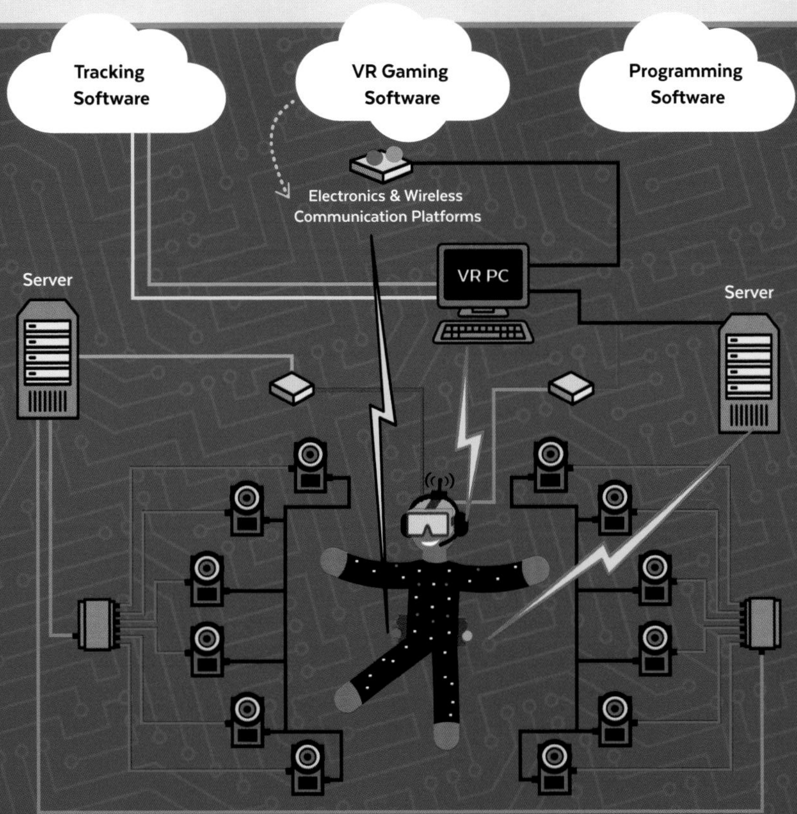

WHAT IS BEING TRACKED?

- voice
- body motion
- respiration
- head position
- smile
- brain activity
- eye movement
- heart rate

Technologies that provide the best user experiences can capture our data and everything we look at and touch. And they can share it to the cloud without our knowing, test our reactions to changing environments and try to influence our decisions.

ADAPTED FROM "HOW TO BUILD AN EMBODIMENT LAB: ACHIEVING BODY REPRESENTATION ILLUSIONS IN VIRTUAL REALITY" © SPANLANG, NORMAND, BORLAND AND KILTENI, GIANNOPOULOS, POMÉS, GONZÁLEZ-FRANCO, PEREZ-MARCOS, ARROYO-PALACIOS, MUNCUNILL AND SLATER, *FRONT. ROBOT. AI*, NOVEMBER 27, 2014. HTTPS://DOI.ORG/10.3389/FROBT.2014.00009

Top leaders in the VR industry came up with ideas to keep VR safe for consumers and still be fair to companies. It's the beginning of many conversations that need to happen, says Jeremy Bailenson.
RAWPIXELIMAGES/DREAMSTIME.COM

LET'S TALK

In 2018 at Stanford University's Virtual Human Interaction Lab, Jeremy Bailenson called a meeting. VR industry leaders were invited to discuss how to address privacy, safety and ethical problems. The goal was to draft a bill of rights for VR consumers, so they would be protected. But the bill also had to be fair to companies, so they could keep inventing technologies. Would it be possible to achieve this balance?

The leaders came up with solutions. One promising idea was to follow the healthcare model. Researchers at universities and hospitals must follow much stricter rules than those working in the industry, to protect the health and safety of patients. And they have committees that review their work to make sure their practices are safe and ethical. The Stanford group hopes healthcare will be a model for the VR industry, and they're working hard to make it happen.

"VR is like uranium: it's this really powerful thing," says Bailenson. "It can heat homes, and it can destroy nations. We can't ignore the darker side, and we each have a role in defining how this technology is shaped and developed."

Researchers Jepsen, Bailenson and Abrash know their technologies are crossing a line. They're advocating for honest, open conversations about how these technologies should be part of our lives and for rules to protect people. They don't want the dangers to stamp out the benefits.

Where's the Line? Young Inventors Speak Out

Can technology go too far? Here's what some young inventors think about BCIs and social VR.

"We have to realize technologies can be used maliciously. They need to be managed, controlled and regulated. And it's the responsibility of people inventing to focus on ethical innovation."

"I feel like living in social VR would have a bad influence on your mental health. It could make you want to be this other person with unachievable abilities. You'd feel like you're never good enough because you couldn't meet the standards of this person that you made yourself."

"They're fantastic for medical care. But when it comes to going mainstream, we need restrictions. I just don't think our society is ready for them, not yet. And the public doesn't know enough about long-term effects."

"I think augmenting intelligence with BCIs raises a lot of ethical problems. Would people understand what's being messed with in their brains? And it'd create inequalities among people. If I could, I definitely would! But we'll need to have a societal debate. The focus must be on making sure everyone has access if they want it."

"BCIs for healthy people to augment themselves pushes my comfort limit. What would be the limit? Humans would never stop pushing the limit. And this is what makes me feel uncomfortable."

"Social VR could empower people if they're struggling with insecurity or disability. But on the other hand, people are at risk of losing touch with reality. It'd be easy to forget who you are. And forget our imperfections as humans."

CHOICES

Science and technology have always shaped human civilization. Important inventions triggered industrial revolutions that changed people's lives and the world. Now we're living through a machine revolution unlike anything before, and we have choices to make.

Past industrial revolutions helped people, but they also hurt them—like when machines took over handmade work and factories sprung up. People could buy more products, and that was good. But when adults and children were forced to work in unsafe factories, that was bad.

TECH_BYTE

Agricultural Revolution
10,000 YEARS AGO:
Foraging to farming changes human culture

First Industrial Revolution
18th & 19th CENTURIES:
Water and steam power mechanizes production

Second Industrial Revolution
19th & 20th CENTURIES:
Electric power creates mass production

Third Industrial Revolution
1960s–2000:
Digital (computer revolution): electronics and information technology automate production

Fourth Industrial Revolution
NOW!
Robotics, AI, Internet of Things, and more are disrupting industry and transforming lives

In 2016 global leaders gathered at the 46th World Economic Forum. Delegates talked about how technological changes were disrupting society. "They're unlike anything that has happened before," said Klaus Schwab. He's an engineer, economist and author with a passion for improving people's lives.

New technologies are "fusing our physical, digital and biological worlds," he said. "They're even challenging our ideas about what it means to be human." Everyone agreed the world has entered into a new era called the Fourth Industrial Revolution (4IR).

"Will the 4IR have a human heart?" Schwab startled everyone with this question.

He thinks it depends on the choices we make. Will we choose to develop and deploy technology that values environmental protection and human rights? What about equality, fairness or safety? If people hold values like these close to their hearts, then the 4IR will have a human heart.

As historian Melvin Kranzberg once said, "Technology's not good, bad or neutral." We shape technology, then it shapes us and on it goes. So we need to think carefully about what technology we put out there in the first place, because once it's out there, we will use it. Where does this situation leave us? Let's ask the experts about designing technology responsibly.

"The Fourth Industrial Revolution should be a revolution of values," says Amira Yahyaoui. She's a human rights activist who runs an organization that safeguards Tunisian citizens' freedom of speech.

REMY STEINEGGER/FLICKR.COM/CC BY-NC-SA 2.0

SET UP!
* Values
* Principles
* Ethics
* Think human
* Rules and laws
* Privacy, safety and security
RISE UP!
* Build trustworthy AI
* Put humans in the loop
* Speak up
* Ask questions
* Look to the future
TEAM UP!
* Diversity and inclusion
* You, me—everyone!

Five

How Do We Design Responsible Technology?

SET UP! RISE UP! TEAM UP!

"Hey! I don't want to build something I'll regret." That's how most designers, engineers and scientists feel. They want their technology to improve people's lives. But projects can go off course for lots of reasons and cause harm.

Maybe it's the thrill of inventing. Maybe they are blinded by the glory of thinking their invention will save the world, or the possibility of making lots of money. Maybe their boss says to skip the safety checks and build it fast. Many things can mess up how designers, engineers and scientists think.

Or maybe they never leave their computer screens in Silicon Valley to talk to other experts or the people who'd use the technology. So they really don't know what's needed, and they are less able to imagine and guard against possible harms.

Working collaboratively leads to better, safer technology.
MASKOT/GETTY IMAGES

Let's say everything goes as planned, and the technology they invent helps people. But years later industries adapt it and use it for different purposes. Once technologies are widely available, inventors can't control how they're developed or used.

For all these reasons and more, people are asking, How do we innovate safely? How can we reap the benefits of wearable technology but still protect against the harms?

The answer lies in *responsible design*!

Designing responsible technology is like doing a puzzle. There are many pieces that need to fit together.

"Move fast and break things"? Not anymore! This motto began with Facebook (now Meta) and gained momentum throughout the tech world. It means innovate fast and don't worry about how technology impacts people. We need to eliminate this mindset and adopt new values, says Tristan Harris.
MATT WINKELMEYER/GETTY IMAGES

SET UP!

Let's start with the basics. Experts agree that values, principles and ethics can help set up a foundation for responsible design. Add in some rules and concern for human well-being, and now you're on a better path to safe innovation!

It's about Values

Tristan Harris is a computer scientist who worked as a design ethicist at Google. Now he heads up the Center for Humane Technology in San Francisco. The center is helping tech makers, companies and governments understand why we end up with harmful technology and how to fix this problem.

He says company values are part of the problem—they're promoting a "move fast and break things" mindset. Tech industries rush forward with innovations. They don't think through how new technologies could affect people. And developers often mistakenly believe that all tech is beneficial.

Not valuing a person's privacy. Believing it's okay to track people's data without them knowing. Values like these are *not* okay! But how do you get industries that are being irresponsible to change their values?

TECH_BYTE

What should I do? What matters most? What do other people think is important? Build the foundation with values, principles and ethics

- **What are values?** Values are *inside* and part of us. They're our beliefs or opinions about things we feel strongly about. Our values can change over time, but along the way, they help us decide what's right and true for us individually. Our values affect how we behave.
- **What are principles?** Principles are *outside* and separate from us. They're like guiding moral rules or natural laws that don't change over time. Fairness is an example of a principle. So is honesty. Principles can help us figure out our values. They can help us make choices when things seem confusing.
- **What are ethics?** What's right or wrong? What's fair or unfair? Ethics are standards for how people should act. They're like our north star or our moral compass. Ethics help us explore and talk about differences between values and principles, and they help us to think about which ones to adopt.

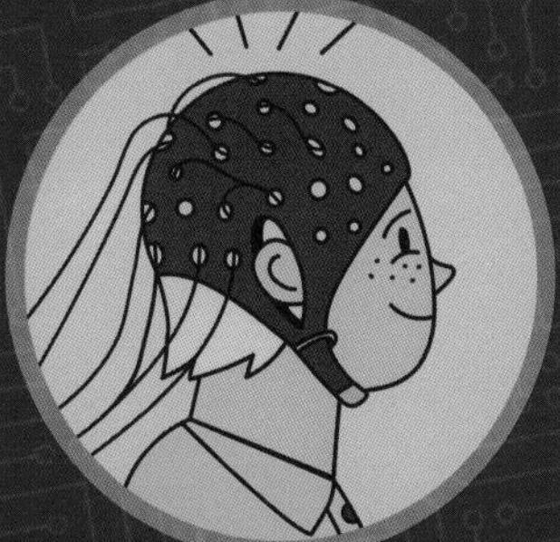

VR can expand educational opportunities. But to make sure this technology is safe and meets kids' needs, experts must adhere to certain principles, such as creating suitable, short field-trip-like experiences and working with teachers who will use the technology.

© UNICEF/HERWIG

It's the Principle of It

Principles can help us rethink our values. That's why Harris and his team came up with a list of human-friendly principles to guide technology design—the idea, for example, that people and their values matter. And that technology's not neutral. People build technologies as tools. We decide whether to make them, how to make and use them or if we should even have them at all. If tech makers use guiding principles like these, they're more likely to innovate responsibly.

The Center for Humane Technology isn't the only group on a responsible-design mission. Many associations, companies and individuals are also using principles to help shape values. Don't track kids—ever! That's Common Sense Media's number one principle.

Common Sense Media is an organization that promotes safe technology and media for children. Never share children's and teens' info without consent! Be open and honest about privacy and security practices! Collect as little personal info as possible, and protect it all!

They're asking tech makers, companies and governments to adopt these guiding principles. Privacy and security should be built into products from the start. And tested at each stage of development.

Ethics and Manmeet's Iron Ring

Around the world, engineers follow a professional code of ethics. "The code is a very, very big thing," says Manmeet Maggu. "Everything we build comes back to ethics." Maggu designed the Trexo robotic legs you read about in chapter 2.

In Canada, when someone receives an engineering degree there's an obligation ceremony. Engineers take an oath to follow an ethical code of conduct. They receive an iron ring to wear on the pinkie finger of their dominant hand.

In the 1900s there was a tragedy. A bridge in Quebec collapsed. Many workers died. The engineers who built the bridge were blamed. One story is that the original iron rings were made of cast iron from the bridge.

"The ring's a powerful symbol of our responsibility," says Maggu. "The idea is that when we write or draw something on paper, the ring's metal scratches the surface. We leave our mark on everything we create." The ring reminds engineers that they're responsible for the technology they bring into the world. And it reminds them to follow the code.

The iron ring engineers wear is a symbol and reminder of the ethics and obligation of their profession.

----PCSTUFF/WIKIMEDIA COMMONS/ CC BY-SA 2.5

MOVE SLOW + THINK HUMAN

Cyborgs! You Need a Code Too

It's not just people who design technology who need an ethical code. If we're all augmented with wearables that can watch and record others, we need a code too, says Steve Mann.

All Tech Makers Need a Code of Ethics

The stakes are high! Computing professionals have a lot of power. They write code that influences everything in society, from the news stories we read to the personal data companies collect. That's why members of the Association for Computing Machinery have an ethical code. It helps them be honest and responsible and sort out right from wrong.

All designers of technology need a code of ethics says Mira Lane. She heads up the Ethics and Society team at Microsoft. "People often don't consider ethics a design problem," she says. "But it is! Especially if their designs have harmful possibilities like destroying someone's privacy or eroding their human rights."

Mike Monteiro agrees. He works at Mule Design in San Francisco. Mike's worried that designers are getting caught up in the "move fast and break things" mindset. He says they need a code too. "It'll help us realize that we're responsible for the technology we put into the world," he says.

Think Human

Engineers and designers solve problems. Values, principles and ethics are important tools in their responsible-design toolbox, but they have other tools too. Engineers use an engineering and design process to guide their problem-solving.

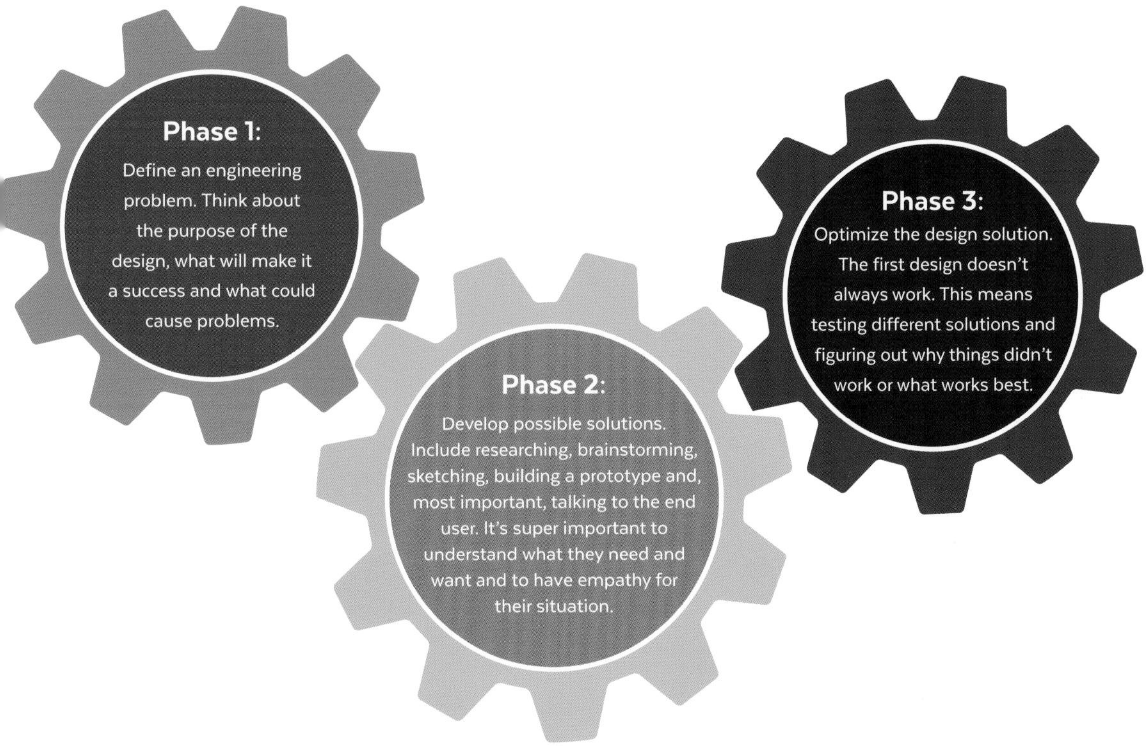

Phase 1:
Define an engineering problem. Think about the purpose of the design, what will make it a success and what could cause problems.
Phase 2:
Develop possible solutions. Include researching, brainstorming, sketching, building a prototype and, most important, talking to the end user. It's super important to understand what they need and want and to have empathy for their situation.
Phase 3:
Optimize the design solution. The first design doesn't always work. This means testing different solutions and figuring out why things didn't work or what works best.

Designers have a guide too. It's a five-step process called human-centered design thinking. But it's more than just steps. It's also a mindset. Designers must understand who they're designing for and what people want and need.

And it's not five steps in order. Designers have to loop backward and forward across the steps until they land on the right design. Human-centered design thinking can help to create wearable devices that are safe and human-friendly and that improve lives.

Whoa! If human-centered design and the engineering and design process help creators think about what people need and want, why do some designs still cause harm? Good question! It's because these guides are only one piece of the responsible-design puzzle.

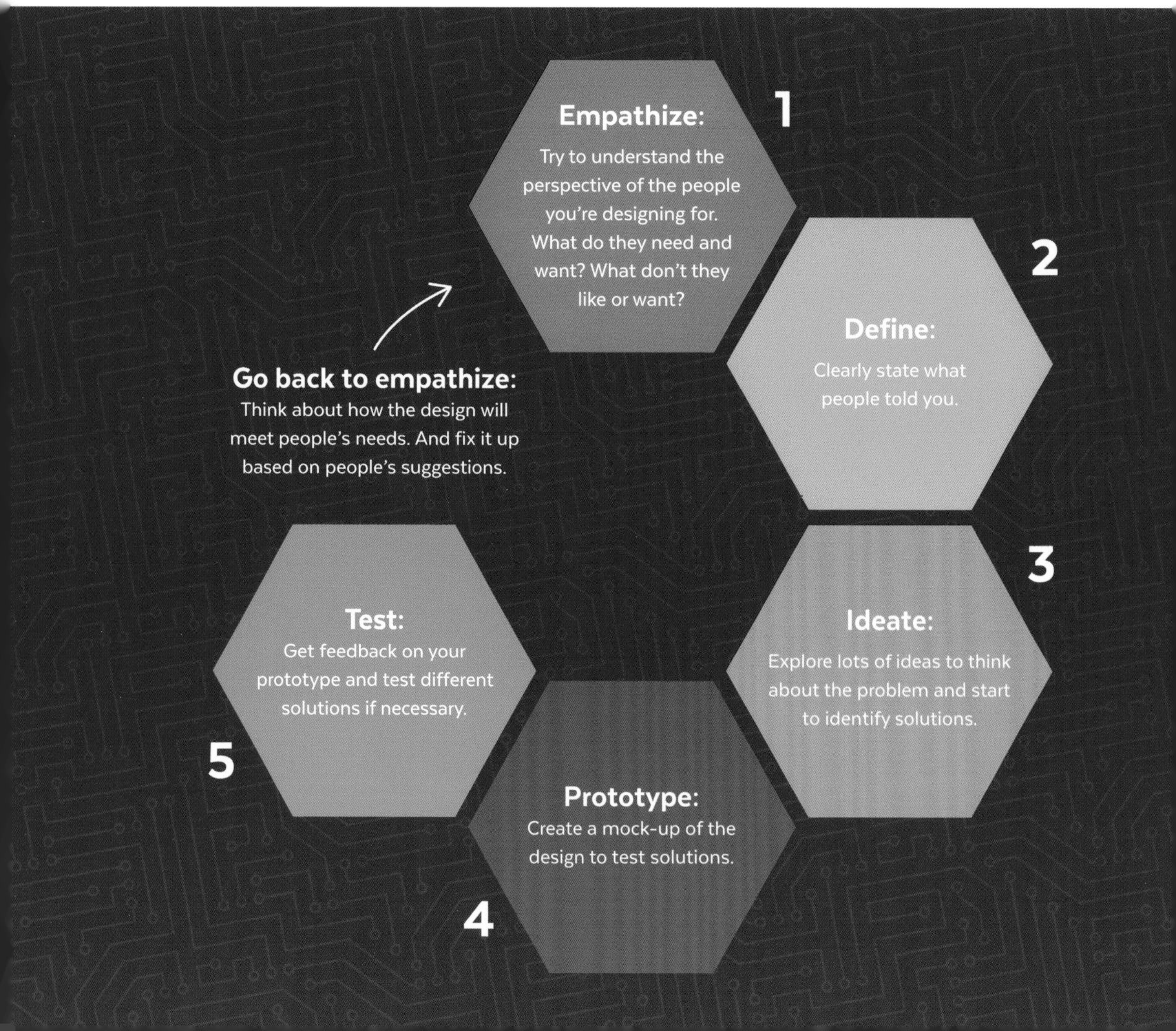

1
Empathize:
Try to understand the perspective of the people you're designing for. What do they need and want? What don't they like or want?
2
Define:
Clearly state what people told you.
3
Ideate:
Explore lots of ideas to think about the problem and start to identify solutions.
4
Prototype:
Create a mock-up of the design to test solutions.
5
Test:
Get feedback on your prototype and test different solutions if necessary.
Go back to empathize:
Think about how the design will meet people's needs. And fix it up based on people's suggestions.

What does it all mean? Do I own my data?
RAWPIXEL.COM/SHUTTERSTOCK.COM

What about Rules and Laws for Wearables?

If we're going to use technologies that collect, store, use and share our information, aren't there rules and laws to keep people safe?

There are, but it's a complicated and confusing patchwork of weak and confusing rules and laws. At least, that's the case in Canada and the United States.

Consumers are confused about what data they own. And they're not sure what information is being collected on them or how companies and governments use and share it.

Click here! People must give their consent when they buy a wearable. That means they understand and agree to privacy policies. They agree to let companies collect, store, use and share their data. But the policies are so long and hard to understand, most people don't read them. They just click *yes* and opt in.

The General Data Protection Regulation ensures that EU citizens own and control their data.

VECTOR IMAGE PLUS/SHUTTERSTOCK.COM

TECH_BYTE

The European Union Leads the World

In 2018 the EU introduced the General Data Protection Regulation. It's a set of principles and rules to protect the personal data of all EU citizens. For example, new privacy measures let people go online to see and control their data. They can even delete it. Companies and individuals worldwide must follow the rules if they collect data on EU citizens. There are severe penalties for violating the rules.

Citizens Want Change!

In 2018 researchers reported that privacy and security concerns are the main reasons people stop using smart wearables. People want to know their personal information is protected and their devices secure. Security is about hackability and reliability.

Governments say it's hard to balance privacy with the tech industry's needs. Too many rules can block their ability to research and innovate. But responsible-design advocates say the government has one main job—to protect its citizens. Companies can't be responsible for regulating themselves.

Good news! Governments and the tech industry realize changes are needed. Some companies are working together and reaching out to government. The EU put strict rules into place. It clamped down on tech companies worldwide. And Denmark was the first country to appoint a tech ambassador to work with the industry.

The Government of Canada is strengthening privacy protections with a new law called the Digital Charter Implementation Act, 2020. Provinces also have laws.

In the United States, each state has privacy laws. California has been a leader with its California Privacy Rights Act of 2020. And there are special laws for health-care and education. Some advocates are calling for a superlaw like the EU has to cover the complicated patchwork of rules and laws to protect privacy.

The Cat-and-Mouse Game

Governments can't make rules and laws fast enough to keep up with the speed of technological developments. It takes a long time to make them, and as soon as they're approved, technologies have changed. There will probably always be a gap. And there will always be some people who find ways around the rules and laws.

For these reasons, companies, schools and universities need to step up to establish values, principles and ethics. Then, we need the force of rules and laws with harsh penalties for violations. And governments need to move faster to catch up to tech developments.

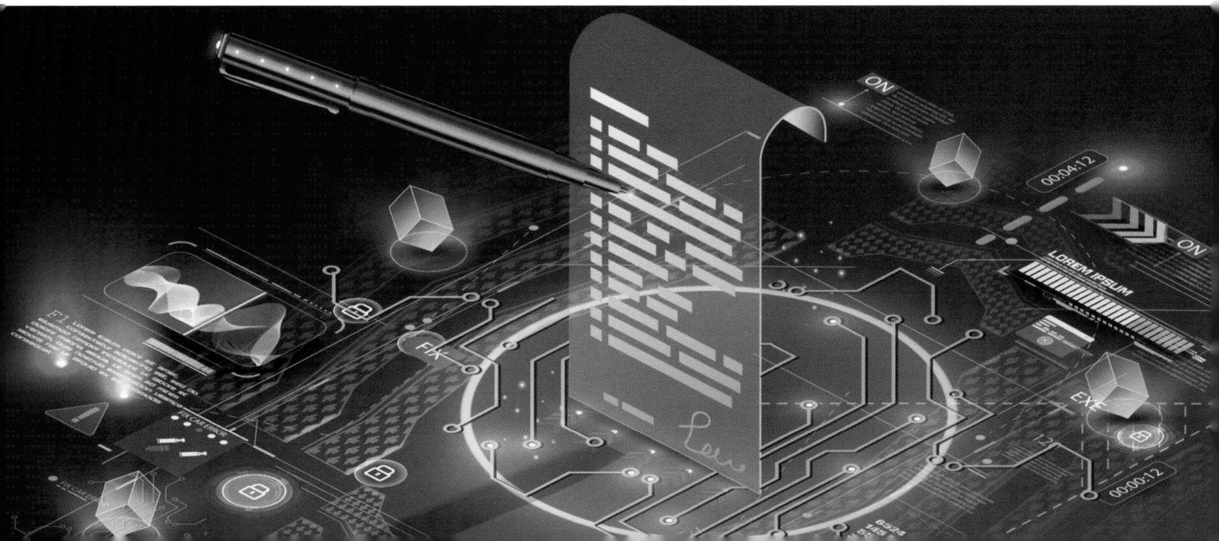

Rules and laws must keep pace with tech developments.

ZINETRON/SHUTTERSTOCK.COM

When Brad Smith of Microsoft spoke to thousands of industry leaders at the 2021 Consumer Electronics Show, they applauded. Smith leads a team of more than 1,500 employees located in 54 countries.

G HOLLAND/SHUTTERSTOCK.COM

RISE UP!

Brad Smith, president and vice chair of Microsoft says we must keep control of the computers we create. "It's up to us," he says. "Tech has no conscience, but people do—we do. And we must exercise our conscience. We must go to work every day and decide how tech will help everyone."

Build Trustworthy AI...and Use Caution

The Open Wearables Initiative is a group of organizations that believe having ***open-source*** software and ***data sets*** can speed up innovation and improve medical care. If the software's open-source, that means it's freely available. Anyone can examine it for "bugs" or mistakes that could put people's privacy, safety and security at risk. Also, researchers can learn from the information if they can share data sets. They can adapt it for their projects instead of starting from scratch. This is a big step forward. It wasn't always the case that people were willing to share this information—it was top secret.

But alarm bells about AI are still ringing. Since AI can process tons of data quickly, companies and governments are using it to make all kinds of decisions, like who qualifies for a bank loan, who goes to jail or who should be accepted into a school. But how do we know the computer is making the right decisions or delivering the right answers? We don't. Responsible-design advocates say algorithms are becoming so complicated that even the best experts find them hard to understand.

And there's another worry too. People design algorithms. People have opinions and ***biases***. Experts are discovering that ***racism***, ***sexism*** and ***discrimination*** are baked into algorithms that are making decisions and affecting lives.

Algorithm Errors Are Bigger Than Wearables

"Justice for the working class!" In 2020 thousands of students in the United Kingdom protested.

When students couldn't write exams in person during the COVID-19 pandemic, UK schools used an algorithm to estimate their marks. The algorithm was based on their past marks and the schools' track record for students getting into university. Historically, more kids from private schools go to university. The computer averaged the data, and brilliant students at public schools in poorer neighborhoods lost their university places. The government apologized and added in grades predicted by teachers. Universities accepted either the algorithm's marks or the teacher's, whichever were highest. They gave students their spots back.

Experts say the UK situation isn't a surprise—biases run deep in society, and algorithms aren't perfect. People select data to train the algorithms. That data might be old, outdated or not accurate. And people's opinions and biases are a part of the data selected. This means technology is reinforcing injustices.

The people who create AI systems don't usually intend to harm. But they need to recognize AI's limitations and the issues of bias. Experts who studied the UK case said the school system lost sight of the main goal. Its job was to help students get to university and go on to find jobs. They should have worked with the universities and government on a different plan for deciding the marks.

In the UK example, experts were able to examine the algorithm, and leaders made changes. That doesn't always happen. Why are schools, governments and companies relying on algorithms to make decisions that have a big impact on citizens? How can we build trustworthy AI systems that are safe, respect privacy and treat everyone fairly? Companies like Microsoft are leading the way and helping others in the tech industry.

Responsible-design advocates are working hard to unlock and examine AI systems. And they're figuring out how to build systems that people can understand.

ALEXANDER LIMBACH/SHUTTERSTOCK.COM

Put Humans in the Loop

How do we want to live with artificial intelligence (AI)? Do we want smart machines that work on their own and take over our abilities? Or do we want them to help us do things better?

Wearables help us collaborate with machines. They can boost our intelligence and abilities. It comes back to researchers Mann, Minsky and Kurzweil and their idea of humanistic intelligence (HI). HI is about designing devices with humans in the loop. If we're part of a computer's decision pathway, we understand how it's working. We also have control over its operations. This gives us power over AI. HI acts as a force to balance AI, and the wearable works better. We'll be good teammates!

Keep AI open! Open-source data and data sets make it possible for researchers to dig in, explore, understand and find ways to prevent bias and create better algorithms—it helps developers and AI systems learn from one another's mistakes.

Humans need to be in the loop in another way too. Even if technology isn't part of us as it is with wearables, AI systems make decisions about us and our lives. An emerging field called explainable AI requires AI systems to tell humans what they are doing and how they are making decisions in a way humans can understand. We need experts to review these decisions and step up when they look unfair. We need to make sure AI systems can't go rogue.

Communication! Let's talk about how AI is affecting our lives.

SKYNESHER/GETTY IMAGES

Speak Up...and Quit?

Right? Wrong? Values, principles and ethics can help tech makers realize a project is wrong. But then what? Every designer needs to speak up and ask questions, says Mule Design's Mike Monteiro. If they realize a project's risky, such as a smart teddy bear for kids that's hackable, they should say, "No, I can't work on this project."

More and more designers are speaking up and quitting. Researchers did a study of tech workers in the United Kingdom. They found that almost 30 percent worried about their company's ethics, and about 20 percent quit over risky projects. When tech makers worked with AI, the study showed that the percentages of people who quit were even higher.

Safety for Everyone

More and more companies are interested in doing the right thing. Many workplaces are encouraging their employees to speak up when they feel something isn't right, because often the irresponsible design is not intentional.

Rebecca George is the past president of BCS, The Chartered Institute for IT. She says we must all ask ourselves questions like, Why am I being asked to do this? Am I doing the right thing? What could be the consequences? But companies need to make it safe for employees to speak out. For example, if an employee at British Airways discovers a safety problem, they're not fired. Instead, there's a celebration.

Rebecca George and BCS, The Chartered Institute for IT are on a mission to lead the information technology industry through its ethical challenges, support the people who work in the industry and make IT good for society.

LEFT: REBECCA GEORGE/BCS, THE CHARTERED INSTITUTE FOR IT

RIGHT: LUIS ALVAREZ/GETTY IMAGES

Yes! This technology works for me.
FOTOSIPSAK/GETTY IMAGES

Step Back, Look Forward

We don't have a crystal ball! say tech makers. How are we supposed to know how our designs will affect people now and in the future? Researchers are developing tools to help them.

Imagine a technology that uses a brain-computer interface to detect a person's emotions. Then it displays those emotions on their shirt sleeve through a smart jacket. The sleeve changes color, texture and shape on the basis of the wearer's feelings. It could help wearers be more aware of their feelings. The people around them would see their feelings too.

Sounds cool, right? Professor Batya Friedman and her team at the University of Washington developed "envisioning cards" to help tech makers talk to people who might use the technology. They might ask, What do you like or not like about the jacket? Would you be concerned if people shared or sold the jacket? What should we plan for?

People might respond with, What happens to my data? Is there a reset button between users? Can I control the settings if I don't want other people to see my emotions? Hearing their comments and questions helps tech makers understand what might worry users. It can prompt designers to fix their designs.

PHOTO VETEROK/SHUTTERSTOCK.COM

TECH_BYTE

Putting the A in STEM

When computer scientist and engineer John Maeda worked as a coder, numbers and rules were his world. One day a kind artist friend told him he was losing touch with humanity.

Later in life, Maeda went to art school. He became more curious and caring about people. He visited Silicon Valley and saw that award-winning companies hired people with art and design skills. When Maeda became president of the Rhode Island School of Design he became a champion for arts and design education, and he talked to the US government about successful innovation. They agreed that schools should follow the same path. So with the addition of the arts, STEM became STEAM.

TEAM UP!

Everyone sees the world differently. That's no surprise! We all have different backgrounds and experiences.

Diversity and Inclusion Make a Difference

Where on the body would a wearable fit best? Should it be customizable? Should the data be available only to the wearer? Do you think everyone would answer these questions in the same way? Most tech-industry leaders agree that they build better, safer products when people with different perspectives, backgrounds, abilities and disabilities come together.

But there's a problem! When you look at who's actually working in tech, there's a lack of diversity and ***inclusion***. Why? Lots of reasons.

Bringing diverse perspectives to tech design leads to better, safer products.
JACOB LUND/GETTY IMAGES

For starters, the tech industry was built mainly by engineers, computer scientists and other developers. People with arts and design backgrounds weren't hired. Fortunately, this situation is changing. Companies realize that people who study things such as art, design, history and English add value—they know how to "humanize" tech.

There's also a long history of women and People of Color not being hired in tech. Women make up less than 30 percent of the technology workforce. Sadly, this is a problem in many countries. The percentage is even lower for People of Color. Racism, sexism, harassment and discrimination have long been a problem in the tech industry.

Not only is this an injustice, but the technology being built doesn't reflect the needs, abilities and values of diverse people. Technology reflects the people who build it.

Companies are doing more to correct injustices. But most people agree that actions to reduce racism, sexism, harassment and discrimination must happen faster.

What's more, governments, schools and the tech sector must work together to make sure that everyone, no matter who they are or where they live, has access to STEAM education and training. There will be millions of tech jobs in the years ahead. They are some of the highest-paying jobs, with the most opportunities. No one should miss out!

Diversity and inclusion must also involve people who will use the technology. Imagine creating a prosthetic limb. For the device to fit and work safely, people who live without limbs should be on the design team.

Tech needs many views! Not only will this make our society more fair, but we'll have better, safer products.

YOU, ME, EVERYONE—WE'RE PART OF THE RESPONSIBLE-DESIGN TEAM

No matter who you are, where you live or what you do, you're part of the responsible-design conversation. Even if you don't build tech, you use it, and you deserve to have a say in what is okay and what is not. Especially *you! Your generation will be the future creators and users of technology!* That might sound like a lot of pressure. But technology's developing faster today than at any other time in history. Thinking about these things now is a big deal. Will wearables shape a better world? Now that you've heard from the experts, it's over to you!

FIRST LEGO League inspires youth through exciting hands-on STEM learning and robotics programs. Encouraging strong teamwork skills is one of *FIRST*'s core values. *FIRST* is about solving big real-world problems *together*.
BRENDON THORNE/GETTY IMAGES

SMART PENCIL
INCOMING HOLOGRAPHIC CALL
ACCEPT
IGNORE
JETSHOE

Get Brainstorming

Can you think of a wearable you'd like to invent? Here are six steps to get started:

1. Ask yourself, Who's the wearable for (the "user")?
2. Be clear about the user's problem. (Why do they want a wearable? What do they want it to do? How will it help them? What don't they want it to do? How could it hurt them? What are the ***criteria*** for success? What are the ***constraints***?)
3. Check the actions below that will help you design responsible technology. You can check as many as you like...even all of them!
   - ☐ Write out your values, principles and ethics.
   - ☐ Know the rules and laws to keep your user safe.
   - ☐ Work in a diverse team to get different points of view.
   - ☐ Talk to a diverse group of people who might use the wearable.
   - ☐ Ask an engineer! Ask a designer! Ask a scientist! Talk to them and other experts about possible harms and how to avoid them.
4. Brainstorm, and explore even the craziest of designs. Draw pictures, do research, build prototypes. Come up with different solutions.
5. Test out your designs. What works? What doesn't work? Why?
6. Go back to the user for their ideas on your solutions. Fix the design.

Ensuring responsible design is a work in progress. It will take some trial and error. You might already be thinking about other pieces to add to the puzzle! Caution! Move slow and think human.

Glossary

algorithm—a set of steps or rules to solve a math problem or complete a computer process

artificial intelligence (AI)—a branch of computer science that studies how to make machines smarter. When machine learning resembles human learning, that's called *strong AI*, or *artificial general intelligence*. When machine learning is focused on doing one kind of task, that's called *weak AI*, or *narrow AI*.

augmented—boosted or improved

biases (singular: bias)—tendencies to favor or be against a particular idea, thing, person or group of people because of personal beliefs

biometric—pertaining to a person's unique physical or behavioral traits. Biometric technology measures and analyzes these traits to identify people. Examples of physical traits are fingerprints, face shape, eye retinas or voice. Behavioral characteristics include how a person sits or walks.

Bluetooth—short-range wireless communication technology that allows devices such as mobile phones, laptops or printers to connect and exchange information

cloud computing—storing data on the internet and sending it to other devices such as computers, smartphones or sensors. Companies provide cloud space on their servers as a service to users.

code—instructions written by people in a way that computers understand, describing the steps a computer program should take

constraints—things that limit what can be done or achieved when designing technology

criteria—standards on which decisions are made. In research, the things a design needs to do or achieve.

cyberspace—the online world of internet-connected computers. Author William Gibson was the first to use the word in his book *Neuromancer*, written in 1984.

cyborg—a human augmented with technological attachments. Authors Manfred Clynes and Nathan Kline invented the word in 1960 in their article called "Cyborgs and Space."

data—in computer science, basic facts that a computer uses to perform tasks or make decisions. Text, emails, apps, pictures, audio clips and other data are processed and stored in numeric code (binary digits with a value of one or zero).

data set—a collection of related data

designers—people who plan and mock up how something will look and work before it's made

discrimination—unfair treatment of a person or group of people on the basis of such characteristics as their race, religion, gender, ability, age or sexual orientation

electrolytes—minerals that carry an electrical charge. They help regulate bodily functions (help our muscles contract, keep us hydrated, etc.). Electrolytes are found in our blood, urine and sweat.

functional near-infrared spectroscopy—technology that uses a special type of light that can go through bone, skin and brain. Scientists and doctors use it to understand how the brain works or diagnose medical problems.

haptic—tactile (relating to the sense of touch). Haptic devices and technology use vibrations, forces and movements to give people the experience of touching a real object.

humanistic intelligence—mental quality that allows for human logic, abstract thought, understanding, self-awareness, communication, learning, emotional knowledge, memory planning, creativity and problem-solving

human-machine symbiosis—humans and machines working interdependently

inclusion—the practice of creating environments that make everyone feel welcome

interfaces—the systems that allow a person to interact with a computer

Internet of Things (IoT)—a system of connected smart devices that can gather, analyze, send and receive data via the internet. Any “thing” can become connected to the web (everyday objects, kitchen appliances, medical implants, television, wearables, etc.).

loop—a set of instructions that tells the computer to repeat a task until it's done

magnetic resonance imaging (MRI)—a diagnostic technique that uses magnetic fields and radio waves to produce computerized images of the internal structure of the brain and other body parts

materials science—the study of the properties of matter to discover how to design and use materials for specific applications

microelectrodes—very small electrodes (electrical conductors that carry electricity) used to study the electrical characteristics of living cells and tissues

microfluidic—pertaining to the study of how very small amounts of fluids behave when they flow through tiny channels. Fluids at a microscale have unique features that make them useful for various science, medicine and technology applications.

open-source—licensing of a software product by its creator to allow its source code (human-readable instructions for a computer program) to be inspected, changed and improved

physiological data—information about a living organism’s functioning, such as a person’s blood pressure, heart rate or brainwave activity

prostheses—substitutes for missing parts of the body. Examples include artificial limbs, eyes, ears and teeth, as well as replacement parts for hearts, kidneys and skin.

prototypes—original or early versions of something built for testing or demonstrating design features

psychological presence—the sensation of “being there” in an environment that doesn't really exist. It’s a basic feature of virtual reality.

racism—the belief that people of certain races, cultures or ethnicities are inferior and therefore deserving of being treated with less kindness, respect and consideration

radio waves—a type of electromagnetic radiation. They're the basic building block of communication technologies such as televisions, radios, mobile phones, satellites, etc. Devices receive radio waves and convert them to mechanical vibrations in the speaker to create sound waves.

sensors—devices that detect and measure physical properties (such as temperature, sound, pressure or movement) in surrounding environments and convert them to a signal that can be read by an instrument or observer

sexism—discrimination based on a person's sex

smart devices—electronic objects that can autonomously gather information about their environments and connect, share data and interact with a user or other devices

smartboards—electronic, interactive whiteboards that display images from a computer screen onto a classroom board via a digital projector

sound waves—waves caused by the vibration of an object going through air, water or a solid medium

Wi-Fi—wireless networking technology, a way of connecting to a computer network using radio waves instead of wires

Resources

PRINT

Bodden, Valerie. *Wearable Technology: Modern Engineering Marvels.* Checkerboard Library, 2018.

Gitlin, Martin. *Smart Wearable Devices.* Cherry Lake Publishing, 2021.

———. *Wearable Electronics*. Cherry Lake Publishing, 2017.

Jackson, Tom. *Future Humans*. QED Publishing, 2019.

Kiffel-Alcheh, Jamie. *Future Tech: The Science Behind the Story.* National Geographic Partners, 2020.

Martin, Brett. *Inside Wearable Technology.* Core Library, 2019.

Otfinoski, Steven. *Making Robots: Science, Technology and Engineering*. Children's Press, 2017.

Reeves, Jordan, and Jen Lee Reeves. *Born Just Right*. Aladdin, 2019.

Reshma, Saujani. *Girls Who Code: Learn to Code and Change the World.* Viking, 2017.

Roland, James. *Changing Lives Through Virtual Reality*. Reference Point Press, 2021.

Stuckey, Rachel. *Designing Inclusive Communities*. Crabtree Publishing, 2018.

ONLINE

Virtual Reality

CNET Virtual Reality 101: cnet.com/special-reports/vr101

Immersive Reality (IR) Books, library ideas: libraryideas.com/ir-books

Introducing VR to Kids workshop by John E. Muñoz: sites.google.com/view/myfirstvrproject/home

Virtual Reality Society: vrs.org.uk

Brain-Computer Interfaces

Mysteries of the Brain: Brain-Computer Interface, video from NBC News Learn and the National Science Foundation

Wearable Robotics

Ekso Bionics (exoskeleton technology): eksobionics.com

Gravity Industries Jet Suit: gravity.co

Lockheed Martin ONYX exoskeleton, video from youtube.com

How I Made a Robot to Help My Nephew Walk, Trexo Robotics, video from ted.com

Sarcos Robotics Guardian XO (powered exoskeleton): sarcos.com

SciTech Now, *Wearable Robots*, season 5 episode 19, video from pbs.org

STEM and STEAM Programs

Center for Neurotechnology: centerforneurotech.uw.edu

FIRST: firstinspires.org

***FIRST* Canada**: firstroboticscanada.org

Frontiers for Young Minds: kids.frontiersin.org

Let's Talk Science, "Design & Build a Wearable Social Distancing Device": letstalkscience.ca

Stanford d.school, "K12 Lab": dschool.stanford.edu

FILM

Brashear, Regan, dir. *Fixed: The Science/Fiction of Human Enhancement*. 2013, Making Change Media. makingchangemedia.com

For a complete list of references, visit the page for this book on our website (orcabook.com).

Acknowledgments

I am extremely grateful to so many people who helped make this book possible. At Orca Book Publishers, my heartfelt thanks to Kirstie Hudson for your insightful comments, kindness, patience and unending enthusiasm for this book. My thanks also go out to the incredible Orca team for bringing this book to life, especially Belle Wuthrich for your fabulous illustrations, Dahlia Yuen for your beautiful design, Vivian Sinclair for copy editing and Georgia Bradburne for editorial assistance.

My deepest gratitude to Jeremy Bailenson, PhD; Jennifer Boger, PhD, PEng; Dean Krusienski, PhD; Steve Mann, PhD, PEng; and Christina Mann (engineer in the making!). Thanks kindly for reviewing the manuscript for accuracy and providing expert insights and thoughtful comments.

Tom Chau, PhD, PEng; Azadeh Kushki, PhD; and Manmeet Maggu, BASc, MBA, I'm ever grateful for your telling me about your projects and sharing wonderful photos. I'm especially indebted to Steve Mann for generously sharing links to sources and remarkable photos, and Jeremy Bailenson for patiently answering my questions and sending information. A huge thanks to John Muñoz, PhD, for letting me visit your spectacular VR lab.

To all the young inventors: a million thanks for telling me about your inventions! Your brilliance and passion for designing technology that will make the world a better place blow my mind! Finn Harding, Grace Jonker, Shane Edelstein, Robin Krasinkiewicz, Soumiya Sivasathiyanathan, Christina Mann, Benjamin Bosworth, Adam Burrell, Sasha Rao, Ethan Toushek, Tommy Hooper, Thomas Gaudet, Ananya Chadha, Samarath Athreya, Shalev Lifshitz, Sabarish Gnanamoorthy, Agosh Saini, Narendra Persaud, Seyon Menakan, Shivani Rajeev, Theipiha Vijayaraj, Varuna Sehgal and Harini Yogeswaran, you're amazing!

I'm incredibly grateful to teachers and the *FIRST* LEGO League coaches for helping me connect with the young inventors. Dave Ellis, Luke Martin, Diana Hale and Barbara Williamson Buckley: thanks to all. Luke, you went above and beyond.

Most sincere thanks to Dana Geall for sharing Brody's story and the fantastic photos.

I also want to acknowledge the magnificent minds who helped me understand wearables and the issues technology is creating for the world.

My heartfelt thanks to mentors and writer friends for helping me shape the book's ideas and cheering me on. Ted Staunton, this book wouldn't be a reality without you! Lisa Dalrymple, Laura Backes Bard, Brian Henry, Peter Lourie, Stephen Swinburne, Rick Wilks, Darlene Ivy, Laurel Neme, Carol Doeringer, Charlotte Blair Jones, Sandra Sutter, Dianna Wilson Sirkovsky, Caterina Salvatori, Sheila Flores and Ashliegh Gehl, I'm ever grateful.

Lastly, my deepest thanks and love to my husband, Michael, and my daughters, Nicole and Allison, for sharing great ideas, being my sounding board and enthusiastically supporting me.

Index

*Page numbers in **bold** indicate an image caption.*

JOHN CARVALHO

ELAINE KACHALA is a health-policy researcher, writer and adviser. She has over 20 years of writing experience with health agencies. *Superpower? The Wearable-Tech Revolution* is her first book. Elaine has a special interest in wearable technologies. She's curious and hopeful but can't help being a little worried about how wearables will impact our health, well-being and equity. With degrees in psychology and sociology from the University of Toronto and a master's degree in environmental studies from York University, she brings a unique perspective to the topic. Elaine lives with her family in Toronto.

ORCA **Think**

THE MORE YOU KNOW THE MORE YOU GROW

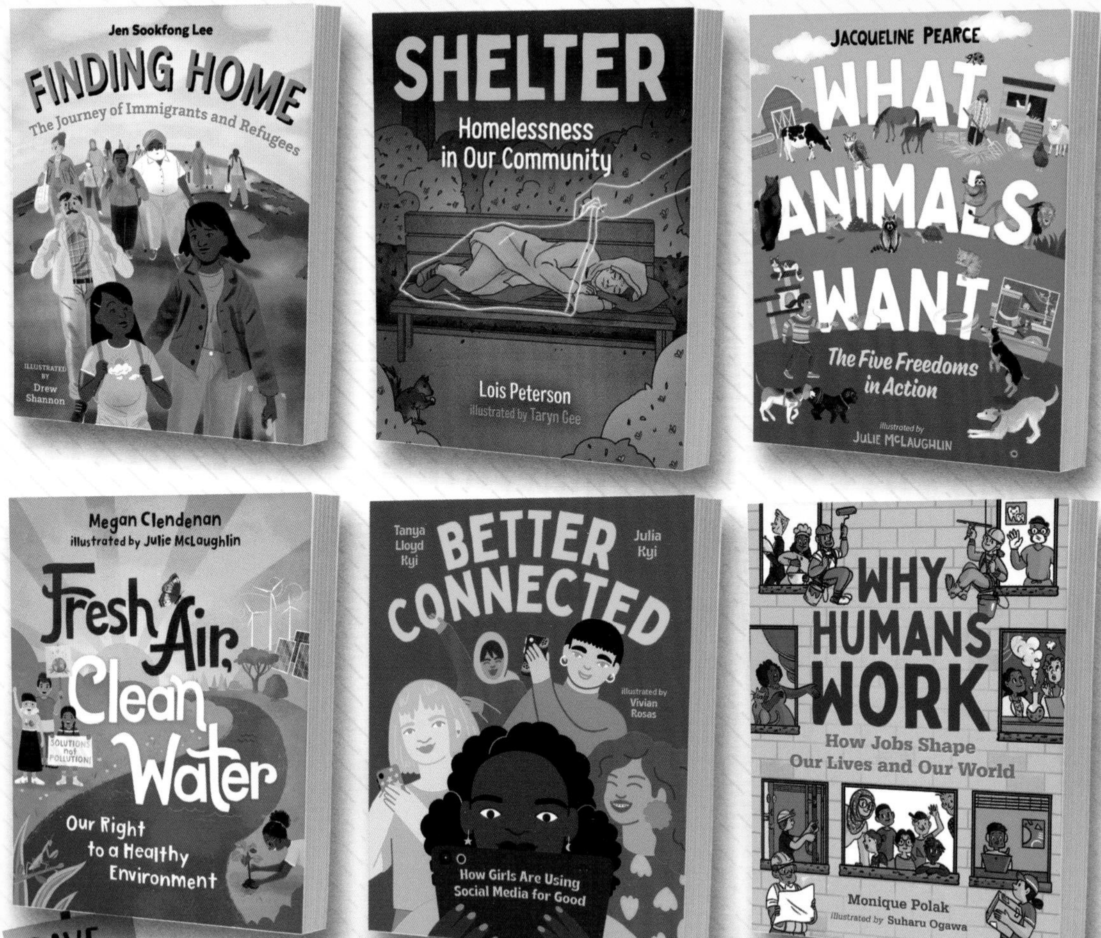

WHAT'S THE BIG IDEA?

The **Orca Think** series introduces us to the issues making headlines in the world today. It encourages us to question, connect and take action for a better future. With those tools we can all become better citizens. Now that's smart thinking!